PORTRAITS FROM THE LIFE OF THE

PROPHET ﷺ MUHAMMAD

COMPILED FROM THE WORKS OF IBN KATHEER, IBN HISHAAM AND OTHER SCHOLARS

TAMIR ABU SU'OOD MUHAMMAD

Qadeem Press

Qadeem Press

Qadeem Press Edition
Breathing Life into Forgotten Pages
www.qadeempress.com

Find our titles on your favourite online bookstore using the keyword 'Qadeem Press'

Publisher's Note

Dar Al-Manarah for Translation, Publishing & Distribution is pleased to present the book, *Portraits from the Life of Prophet Muhammad,* peace and blessings be upon him. The book aims to offer our readers a comprehensive coverage of the biography of the most venerable Prophet, Muhammad, peace and blessings be upon him, and to help demonstrate the excellent example he showed in calling people to the path of Islam, as well as the great tribulations he went through.

We are also grateful to the author and the editor for their relentless effort clearly manifested all through the book.

Finally, all praise and thanks are due to Allah, without whose Help and Guidance nothing can be accomplished.

Publisher Muhammad `Uthmaan

Table of Contents

Chapter One: The Early Days

Chapter Two: Muhammad Chosen Prophet

Chapter Three: The Prophet Establishes the Muslim State

Chapter Four: The Prophet on the Battlefield

Foreword

In the Name of Allah, Most Gracious, Most Merciful

All praise and thanks are due to Allah, the Lord of the Worlds. I praise Him, seek His Forgiveness and Assistance. I seek refuge in Allah from the evils within myself and the evils of our bad deeds. I bear witness that there is no god but Allah; He is alone without any associate, and I bear witness that Muhammad is His Messenger and bondman, may Allah's Peace and Blessings be upon him, his kith and kin, his Companions, those who call to his message and follow his guidance until the Day of Judgment.

Almighty Allah says in the Qur'an:

﴿إِنَّ اللَّهَ وَمَلائِكَتَهُ يُصَلُّونَ عَلَى النَّبِيِّ يَا أَيُّهَا الَّذِينَ آمَنُوا صَلُّوا عَلَيْهِ وَسَلِّمُوا تَسْلِيمًا {٥٦}﴾ (الأحزاب:٥٦)

"Allah and His Angels send blessing on the Prophet: o ye that believe send ye blessings on him, and salute him with all respect." (Al-Ahzaab: 56)

Muhammad, peace and blessings be upon him! This noble name has been on the lips of countless of men. For almost fourteen centuries, millions of hearts have palpitated with deep emotion at the pronouncement of it. Whenever his name is proclaimed through minarets we rejoice, as do the dead and other spiritual beings. Many more millions of people will eternally pronounce it, and will be deeply moved by it.

Of all Allah's Prophets and Messengers, the resplendent glory of the achievements of Prophet Muhammad has remained undimmed over the past fourteen centuries. Unfortunately, the Western world's understanding of him remained wraped for many centuries because of the hostile propaganda and the persistent attacks waged against Islam. During the Crusades, all sorts of slanders were leveled against Prophet Muhammad. With the birth of the modern age, characterized by a greater degree of religious tolerance and freedom of thought, some sort of a change of hearts and approach has been witnessed from some Western authors who study the Prophet's life and characters. Allah be thanked that during the second half of the twentieth Century, far more literature on Islam, the Prophet and related Islamic themes has appeared in the West than ever before. Most of this literature has unbiased and positive contents, which give the non-Muslim readers in the West a better understanding of Islam than in bygone centuries.

For the past fourteen centuries, many

thinkers, philosophers, scientists and prominent scholars in our intellectual world have stood behind Prophet Muhammad, peace and blessings be upon him, in respect and admiration and taken pride in membership of his community. In his book, *The Life and Teachings of Muhammad*, Annie Besant writes: "It is impossible for anyone who studies the life and character of the great Prophet of Arabia, who knows how he taught and how he lived, to feel anything but reverence for that mighty Prophet, one of the great messengers of the Supreme. And although in what I put to you I shall say many things which may be familiar to many, yet I myself feel whenever I re-read them, a new way of admiration, a new sense of reverence for that mighty Arabian teacher.[1]

Also W Montgomery is quoted to have written about Muhammad: "His readiness to undergo persecution for his beliefs, the high moral character of the men who believed in him and looked up to him as leader, and the greatness of his ultimate achievement all argue for his fundamental integrity. To suppose Muhammad an impostor raises more problems than it solves. Moreover, none of the great figures of history is so poorly appreciated in the West as Muhammad.[2]

[1] Annie Besant, *The Life and Teachings of Muhammad,* Madras, 1932, p.4.)
[2] W Montgomery Watt, *Muhammad At Mecca*, Oxford, 1953, p 52.)

As should be expected, there are some books and other publications which present a negative and bias-ridden picture of Islam and Islamic history. Cobweb of misunderstanding still persist in some parts of the West about Islam. Unfortunately, the West still has not realized the splendor of nor have they grasped the clear vision beamed to them about Prophet Muhammad, peace and blessings be upon him: he is the last of the Prophets sent by Allah to guide mankind to the truth. In spite of its great advances in other areas of life, the West still has not made a sincere and objective attempt to understand the message brought by the Prophet. Although some people have seen him as a person worthy of high praise and have paid him glowing tributes on the levels of personal integrity and achievement, his noble status as the Prophet of God has almost been unreasonably rejected, either explicitly or implicitly, by the West. Time is now ripe to treat this with a spirit of true objectivity and open-mindedness.

It is the duty of conscientious Muslims and their fair-minded non-Muslim friends to help remove these misunderstandings and misconceptions through inter-faith dialogue, person-to-person communication and informative books and publications.

This was, in fact, the method used by Prophet Muhammad himself to propagate Islam and spread the Word of Allah. In a world which is shrinking rapidly into a Global Village, we, Muslims, have to endeavor to build bridges of amity and concord with non-Muslim communities in a spirit of co-existence and stress the fact that Islam and the teachings of its Prophet seek the good of the entire human race.

I feel profoundly privileged in being able to present this small treatise, *Portraits from the Life of Prophet Muhammad,* which aims to introduce the reader to the exemplary life of the blessed Prophet, Muhammad, peace and blessings be upon him, and his distinguished, exalted personality. It was firstly published in the year 2000 as part of the book , *Stories of the Prophets,* also translated by me in conjunction with others, and now it is to my pleasure that this part is published as a separate book.

I pray to Almighty Allah to accept this effort as a good deed done solely for His Sake, and to help the reader benefit from it. Amen.

Tamir Abu As-Su`ood

Abbreviations Used:

AC After Christ
AH After Hijrah

Transliteration of Arabic Words and Names:

The following table shows the system followed in transliterating the letters of the Arabic alphabet:

	A	T	
	Aa (long vowel)	Z	ظ
ب	B	` (inverted apostrophe)	ع
ت	T	Gh	غ
ث	Th	F	ف
ج	J	Q	ق
ح	H	K	ك
خ	Kh	L	ل
د	D	M	م
ذ	Dh	N	ن
ر	R	H	ه
ز	Z	W (consonant)	و
س	S	Oo (long vowel)	
ش	Sh	y (consonant)	ى
ص	S	Ee (long vowel)	
ض	D	' (apostrophe)	ء

The Early Days

Name and Lineage:

Muhammad, peace and blessings be upon him, as the majority of biographers state, is the son of `Abdullaah, son of `Abdul-Muttalib, son of Haashim, son of `Abdu Manaaf, son of Qusayy, son of Kilaab, son of Murrah, son of An-Nadr, son of Kinaanah, son of Uzaymah, son of Mudrikah, son of Elyas, son of Mudar, son of Nizaar, son of Ma`dd, son of `Adnaan. His mother, Aaminah, was the daughter of Wahb. His father died while his mother was still pregnant. His grandfather then took charge of him.

His Birth and Nursing:

The Prophet, peace and blessings be upon him, was born in Makkah (Mecca). The exact date of his birth is disputed[1], but it is most likely to be on Monday, 9th Rabee` Al-Awwal (20th or 22nd of April,

[3] This uncertainty concerning birthdates is quite common in Arabia, ***"the country of the illiterate people,"*** as the Qur'an called it. Even nowadays, it is so difficult to date the birth of famous men; for example, it is hard to establish the exact birthdate of well-known king `Abdul `Azeez bin Su`ood, the conqueror and unifier of Arabia, a man who ruled for more than fifty years, and whose personality, conduct and biography are known in great detail.

571 AC), the same year in which the invasion of the Elephants took place against the Ka`bah.

After the Prophet's birth, his mother sent for his grandfather `Abdul-Muttalib to tell him that she had given birth to a boy and asked him to come and see him. Ibn Ishaaq narrates: Abdul-Muttalib took the baby and entered the Ka`bah, where he stood and prayed to Allah showing gratitude to Him for this gift. He then named him Muhammad, a rather uncommon name among the Arabs, and circumcised him on the seventh day of his birth, according to the traditions of Quraysh at that time. He then tried to find a wet nurse for him.

A Bedouin woman called Haleemah Bint Abu Dhu'ayyib was asked to nurse Prophet Muhammad, peace and blessings be upon him. He was thus brought up in a typical Bedouin environment and spoke pure Arabic His foster-brother was `Abdullaah Ibn Al-Haarith; Unaysah and Hudhaafah (or Judhaamah) were his foster-sisters. The Prophet's foster-father was Al-Harith Ibn `Abdul-`Uzzah.

Ibn Ishaaq quotes Haleemah as narrating the following: I departed from my country along with my husband and little son whom I was nursing, in the company of the women of my tribe, in search of other babies to nurse. That was a year of drought when we had nothing left. I was riding a dusky she-donkey of mine with an old she-camel that could not yield a drop of milk. Our hungry child kept us awake all night with his weeping. I hardly had not milk in my breast to feed him, nor could our she-camel provide his morning bowl, but we were hoping for rain and relief. I rode my donkey that was far behind the other riders on account of its weakness and emaciation so that it was a nuisance to them. When we reached Makkah, we looked out for nurslings, and the Prophet of Allah was offered to everyone of us, yet each woman refused him when she was told he was an orphan, as we were hoping for some favor from the baby's father. "An orphan!" We exclaimed, "What will his mother and grandfather do for us?" And so we spurned him because of that. Every woman who came with me got a baby to suckle except me, and when we decided to depart, I said to my husband, "By Allah, I do not like to return in the company of my friends without having taken a babe to suckle; I will go and take that orphan." "Do as you like," he replied, "perhaps Allah will bless us on his account." So I went back and took him for no reason save that I could find none but him. No sooner had I held him in my arms than my breasts overflowed with milk for him. He drank his fill, as did his foster-brother. Then both of them had a good deep sleep, whereas we could not sleep before because of his incessant wailing. My husband got up and went to the old she-camel, and to his total amazement, her udders were full. He milked her and we drank of her milk to our heart's content, and we spent a happy night. In the morning, my husband said to me, "By Allah, Haleemah, you have taken a blessed creature!" "By Allah, I hope so," I said. Then we went out. As I was riding my she-donkey and carrying him with me, she outstripped the other donkeys and they could not keep pace with her to the point that my companions said to me, "Confound you! Stop and wait for us. Is not this donkey of yours the same one you did come on?" "Certainly it is," I replied. They said, "By Allah, something extraordinary had happened." Then we came to our dwellings in the Banu Sa`d country and I know of no place on Allah's earth more barren than that then was. But after we had brought him (the Prophet) to live with us, my flock used to yield milk in abundance. We milked them and drank while other people had not a drop, nor could they find any in their animals' udders so that our neighbors would say to their shepherds, "Out upon you! Send your flock to graze where the daughter of Abu Dhu'ayyib's shepherd goes." Even so, their flocks would came home hungry, yielding no milk, while mine would come back with milk in plenty. We realized that that bounty came from Allah for a period of two years, when I weaned him. He was growing up well and none of the other babies could match him. By the time he was two, he was a well-built child. We brought him to his mother, though we were most eager to keep him with us because of the blessing he brought us. So I said to her, "May you leave my little boy with me until he becomes stronger, for I worry about him from the pest in Makkah." We importuned her until she gave him once more into our keeping.

Purifying the Prophet's Heart:

Few months later, the Prophet was with his foster-brother shepherding the lambs behind the tents when his brother came running to Haleemah and said, "Two men clothed in white have seized the Qurayshite brother of mine, laid him down, opened up his breast, and are stirring it up." So they ran towards him and found him on his feet with his face so livid. They then drew him closer and asked him what the matter was. He said, "Two men in white raiment came to me, laid me down, tore open my breast and searched therein for I know not what."

Describing the event, the Prophet, peace and blessings be upon him, said: "*There came to me Gabriel while I was playing with my foster-brothers, and seized me and opened up my breast, extracted my heart and split it; then he extracted a black clot from it and cast it away saying, 'This is the share of Satan in you.' Then he washed my heart in a gold basin full of water from Zamzam until he had cleaned it. Then he returned it to its place."*

Concerning this incident, Allah says:

﴿أَلَمْ نَشْرَحْ لَكَ صَدْرَكَ {١} وَوَضَعْنَا عَنكَ وِزْرَكَ {٢} الَّذِي أَنقَضَ ظَهْرَكَ {٣} وَرَفَعْنَا لَكَ ذِكْرَكَ {٤}﴾ (الشرح: ١-٤)

"Have we not expanded thee thy breast? And removed from thee the burden that which gall thy back? And raised high the esteem (in which) thou (art held)?" (Ash-Shar<u>h</u>: 1-4)

Out of fear on his account, Haleemah took the Prophet back to his mother and he lived with her until he became six years of age. Upon her return from a visit with the Prophet to her husband's grave, she died in Abwaa` between Makkah and Madeenah (Medina). Thus the Prophet was left to his grandfather. Ibn Hishaam narrates: His grandfather made him a bed in the shade of Ka`bah. His sons used to sit round the bed until he came out to it, but none of them sat upon it out of respect for him. The Prophet, still a little boy, used to come and sit on it and his uncles would drive him away. When `Abdul-Mu<u>tt</u>alib saw this, he said, "Let my son alone, for by Allah a great future is in store for him." There he would have him sit beside him on his bed and would stroke his back with his hand. It used to please him to see what he did.

The Death of `Abdul-Muttalib:

When the Prophet was eight, his grandfather died. Upon his demise, the Prophet's guardianship was passed to his Uncle Abu Taalib whose love for and protection of Muhammad continued long after the Prophet proclaimed his mission and declared the new faith.

When the Prophet was twelve, he accompanied his uncle on a trade mission to Syria. When the caravan reached Busra in Syria, there was a monk there in his cell by the name of Baheerah, who was well-versed in the knowledge of Christianity. Looking at the Prophet, Baheerah asked Abu Taalib, "Who is this boy? " "He is my son," replied Abu Taalib. "He is not," Baheerah said, "for it could not be that this boy's father is alive." "He is my nephew," Abu Taalib answered correctingly. "Then what of his father?" asked Baheerah. "He died," answered Abu Taalib. "You have told the truth", said Baheerah. "Take your nephew back to his country and guard him carefully against the Jews, for by Allah, if they see him and know about him what I know, they will do him evil; a great future awaits this nephew of yours, so take him home now." Abu

Taalib took the Prophet off quickly and returned to Makkah.

Thus the Prophet, peace and blessings be upon him, grew up protected by Allah, Who guarded him against the vileness of disbelief because He wished to honor him with Prophethood, until he grew up to be the finest of his people in manliness, the best in character, the most noble in lineage, the best neighbor, the kindest, most truthful, most reliable young man, the furthest removed from filth and corrupt morals, through loftiness and nobility, so that he was renowned among his people as the Trustworthy (As-Saadiq Al-Ameen) because of the good qualities Allah had instilled in him.

The Prophet's Participation in *Harb Al-Fujjaar* (the Sacrilegious War):

When the Prophet, peace and blessings be upon him, turned fifteen, a sacrilegious war broke out between the two tribes of Kinaanah and Qays `Aylaan. It was so called because the two tribes fought in the sacred month. At the beginning of the war, Qays had the upper hand but by midday Kinanah were victorious. It is mentioned that the Prophet, peace and blessings be upon him, took part in that war.

The Prophet's Membership in *Hilf Al- Fudool* (the Pact of Chivalry):

The Prophet, peace and blessings be upon him, was a member in the pact called *Hilf Al-Fudool*, which aims at protecting the defenseless and ensure safety for strangers in Makkah. The pact first originated because a stranger from Yemen sold goods in Makkah to an influential member of a powerful local clan who subsequently refused either to pay the price or to return the goods, whereupon the aggrieved seller stood up in the vicinity of the Ka`bah and implored people to come to his rescue, being a stranger in the city. Several members of Quraysh's aristocracy rallied to assist him and secured the return of his goods. Meeting next in the Ka`bah at the house of `Abdullaah Ibn Jud`aan, they pledged henceforth to combat oppressive acts and uphold justice. Muhammad, then only twenty-five years old, was present at this gathering, and was so impressed with the merits of the pledge that when he commenced his mission, he legalized it in Islam. As years went by, even after his mission had become a success, the Prophet continued to express both his high regards for the pact and his willingness to abide by its provisions.

Muhammad Chosen Prophet

The Prophet Marries Khadeejah

Ibn Ishaaq narrates: Khadeejah was a merchant woman of dignity and wealth. It had been her custom to hire men to carry merchandise outside the country on a profit-sharing basis, for Quraysh were people given to commerce. She heard much good about the truthfulness, trustworthiness and honorable character of the Prophet, peace and blessings be upon him, so, she sent word to him, asking him to go on a trade caravan taking her goods to Syria to trade in them, while she would pay him more than she paid the others. He was to take along a lad of hers called Maysarah. The Prophet, peace and blessings be upon him, accepted the proposal, and the two set off with her goods to Syria.

The Prophet took shelter under the shade of a tree near a monk's cell. The monk came up to Maysarah and asked him, "Who is the man resting beneath the tree?" Maysarah told him that he belonged to the tribe of Quraysh, the people who had guardianship of the Sanctuary. Thereupon the monk exclaimed, "None but a Prophet ever sat under this tree."

Then the Prophet sold the goods he had

brought, bought what he wanted to buy and set out on journey back to Makkah. The story goes that at the height of noon when the heat was intense as he rode his beast, Maysarah saw two angels shading the Prophet from the sun. Upon reaching Makkah, they brought Khadeejah her property. She sold it and it amounted to double or thereabouts. Maysarah for his part told her about the two angels who shaded him and of the monk's words.

Now Khadeejah was a determined, noble, and intelligent woman possessing the proper ties with which Allah willed to honor her. So when Maysarah told her of these things, she sent to the Prophet. When he came, she said, "O son of my uncle, I love you for your kinship to me, and for that your are ever in the center; and I love you for your trustworthiness and for your nobility and truthfulness." Then she proposed marriage.

The Prophet, peace and blessings be upon him, told his uncles of Khadeejah's proposal, and his uncle Hamzah `Abdul-Muttalib went with him to Khuwaylid, Khadeejah's father, and asked for her hand in marriage and the Prophet married her.

Khadeejah was the mother of all the Prophet's children except Ibraheem, namely Al-Qaasim, At-Taahir, At-Tayyib, Zaynab, Ruqayyah, Umm

Kulthoom and Faat̲imah. Al-Qaasim, At̲-Tayyib, and At̲-Taahir died before Islam. All his daughters lived into Islam, embraced it, and migrated with him to Madeenah.

The Prophet Receives the Qur'an

The Mother of the Believers, `Aa'ishah, may Allah be pleased with her, narrates: The first aspect of revelation unto Allah's Prophet was that his dreams always came true. Whatever vision he would have in his sleep would occur exactly as he had seen. Then, he began to enjoy seclusion. He used to retreat alone into the Cave of Hire` where he would spend several days in devotion before going back to his family. He used to take some provisions with him, and when he returned home, he would take a fresh supply for another period. He continued to do so till he received the truth while in the Cave of Hire`. The angel (Gabriel) came to him and said, "Read". He replied, "I am not a reader". The Prophet says, "*He held me and pressed hard till I was exhausted, then he released me and said, "Read", and I replied, "I am not a reader." So, he held me and pressed me hard for the third time. Then he said:*

﴿اقْرَأْ بِاسْمِ رَبِّكَ الَّذِي خَلَقَ {١} خَلَقَ الْإِنسَانَ مِنْ عَلَقٍ {٢} اقْرَأْ
وَرَبُّكَ الْأَكْرَمُ {٣} الَّذِي عَلَّمَ بِالْقَلَمِ {٤} عَلَّمَ الْإِنسَانَ مَا لَمْ يَعْلَمْ
{٥}﴾ (العلق: ١-٥)

"Proclaim (or Read!) In the name of thy Lord and Cherisher, Who created - created man, out of a (mere) clot of congealed blood: Proclaim! And thy lord is Most Bountiful, - He Who taught (the use of) the Pen, - taught man that which he knew not." (Al `Alaq: 1-5). Trembling, the Prophet rushed home to Khadeejah and said, "Wrap me! Wrap me!" They wrapped him and after a while his fear subsided. He turned to Khadeejah and exclaimed, "What has happened to me?!" He then told her of his experience and commented, "I feel for myself". Thereupon, Khadeejah reassured him, "Never fear, everything will be all right. Allah will never let you down; you are kind to your relatives, you are patient and astute, you assist anyone in need, you are hospitable to your guests, and you help in every just cause." Khadeejah then took him to Waraqah Ibn Nawfal, her paternal cousin who was a Christian convert and a scholar well-versed in Arabic, Hebrew, and the Gospel. He lost his eyesight as he had grown very old. Khadeejah said to Waraqah, "Cousin, would you like to hear what your nephew has to say? "Well, nephew," Waraqah said, "what have you seen?" The Prophet narrated to him what he had seen. When he finished, Waraqah said, "It is the same revelation (*Namoos*) as was sent down to Moses, peace and blessings be upon him. I wish I was a young man so that I might be alive when your people force you out of your city." "Would they force me out?" The Prophet exclaimed. "Yes!" Waraqah answered, "no man has ever come with a revelation like yours but was met with enmity and persecuted." Waraqah continued, " If I live till that day, I will certainly give you all my support." But Waraqah died soon after that and the revelation lingered.

After a short interlude, the Prophet, peace and blessings be upon him, again heard the same voice calling him, "Muhammad, you are the Messenger of Allah, and I am Gabriel." Rushing back to Khadeejah in a state of extreme exhaustion, he asked her to cover him with a cloak. Then he heard the call:

﴿ يا أيها المُدَثّرُ {١} قُمْ فأنذِرْ {٢} وَرَبَّكَ فكَبِّرْ {٣} وثيابك فطَهِّرْ {٤}وَالرجز فاهْجُرْ {٥} ولا تَمْنُن تَسْتَكْثِرُ {٦} ولِرَبِّكَ فاصْبِرْ {٧}﴾ (المدّثر: ١-٧)

"***O thou wrapped up (in a mantle)! Arise and deliver thy warning! And thy Lord do thou magnify! And thy garments keep free from stain! And all abomination shun! Nor expect, in giving, any increase (for thyself)! But, for thy Lord's (Cause) be patient and constant!***"(Al-Muddaththir: 1-7)

Muhammad Assumes His Prophetic Office

It was then that the Prophet, peace and blessings be upon him, realised what his mission to his people was to be, and that was how it began. He began to respond to Allah's command: he started calling on his people to the worship of Allah solely and the renunciation of idol-worship. In the beginning, he preached his message secretly lest the polytheists in Quraysh should hear about him. He started by inviting his nearest kins and intimate friends. He won over few converts: his wife Khadeejah, `Ali Ibn Abi Taalib, Zayd Ibn Haarithah, Abu Bakr As-Sideeq, `Uthmaan Ibn `Affaan, Az-Zubayr Ibn Al-`Awwaam, `Abdur-Rahmaan Ibn `Awf, Sa`d Ibn Abi Waqqaas etc., may Allah be pleased with them all.

The new converts used to meet the Prophet secretly, and when one of them wanted to perform acts of worship, he/she would go to the glens of Makkah where they could observe them out of the polytheists' sight. When the number of Muslims reached thirty, the Prophet, chose the house of Al-Arqam Ibn Abi Al-Arqam to be a teaching place and place of worship as well. Muslims used to go there from time to time to learn about Islam from the Prophet, peace and blessings be upon him.

The Prophet Preaches Islam Publicly:

Three years passed since the beginning of the revelation, during which people began to embrace

Islam in large numbers and the star of Islam started to grow brighter and higher by the day all across Makkah. Then Allah addressed the Prophet, peace and blessings be upon him, with these words,

﴿وَأَنذِرْ عَشِيرَتَكَ الْأَقْرَبِينَ {٢١٤}﴾ (الشعراء: ٢١٤)

"And admonish thy nearest kinsmen..." (Al Shu`araa': 214)

Having received Allah's command, the Prophet gathered his relatives and said, "O sons of `Abdul-Muttalib, I know of you Arab who has come to his people with a nobler message than mine. I have brought you the best of this world and the next. Allah has commanded me to call you unto Him. So which of you will help me in this matter, and be my brother, My executor and my successor? " The first one to answer the call was `Ali Ibn Abi Taalib.

Soon after this command, the Prophet was again addressed:

﴿فَاصْدَعْ بِمَا تُؤْمَرُ وَأَعْرِضْ عَنِ الْمُشْرِكِينَ {٩٤}﴾ (الحجر: ٩٤)

"Therefore expound openly what thou art commanded, and turn away from those who join false gods with Allah." (Al Hijr: 94)

For the first time, the Prophet stood on the mountain of As-Safa opposite the Ka`bah and said to the people, "Supposing I now told you that just behind the slopes of this mountain there was an enemy cavalry preparing to attack to you. Would you believe me?" "We know that you never lie," they replied. Thereupon, the Prophet said: "I warn you that I have a message from Allah, and I have come to you as a warner of a dreadful punishment. I cannot protect you in this world, nor can I promise you anything in the Hereafter, unless you bear witness that there is no god but Allah, the one and only God." On hearing this statement, Abu Lahab flared up and cursed the Prophet, saying, "Perdition to thee." Then Allah said concerning him,

﴿تَبَّتْ يَدَا أَبِي لَهَبٍ وَتَبَّ {١}﴾ (المسد: ١)

"Perish the hands of the Father of Flame! Perish he!"(Al-Masad: 1)

Quraysh Take Action

Having realized that the call of Muhammad was directed against their gods and their inveterate practices, Quraysh decided to take action. If the idols were destroyed, what would become of them, being the keepers of idols? What would become of their renown throughout the land? Some of their leaders went to Abu Taalib and said, "O Abu Taalib, your nephew has cursed our gods, insulted our religion, mocked our ways of life and accused our fathers of error; either you stop him or you let us get at him." However, he gave them a soft answer and they went away.

The Prophet continued to spread Allah's religion and to call on men to worship Him. When Quraysh saw that Abu Taalib had done nothing to stop his nephew or to dissuade him from persisting in what he was doing, they went over to him again and said: "O Abu Taalib, yours is a high and honorable position amongst us, and we have asked you to hold in check your nephew's activities, but you have not done so. By Allah, we cannot tolerate that our fathers should be insulted, our customs scoffed at, and our gods reviled. Either you make him desist or we will fight the pair of you until one side perishes."

Afraid on the Prophet's account, Abu Taalib sent for him and told him, "O my nephew, spare me and yourself. Do not lay on me a burden greater than I can bear." To this the Prophet said: "O my uncle, by Allah, if they were to place the son on my right hand and the moon on my left on the condition that I renounce this Message, until Allah has made it victorious, or I perish instead, I would never renounce it." Then the Prophet, with tears in his eyes, rose to his feet and turned to depart, but his uncle called him back. "Son of my brother," he said, "go and say what you believe; by Allah, I will never, under any circumstances, let you down."

The Persecution of the Prophet and His Followers:

It was then, when the Prophet began to spread his religion and speak against gods, that Quraysh became actively hostile, persecuting his followers, mocking and insulting him. The one consideration which prevented them from killing him was fear from the blood-vengeance of the clan to which the Prophet, peace and blessings be upon him, belonged. However, the Prophet kept proclaiming his message and forsaking their idols, while Quraysh did all they could to ridicule his teachings and deject his followers. The Prophet was called a poet, a sorcerer, a diviner, and a madman.

One day, when the leaders of Quraysh were sitting in the Sacred House, the Prophet entered and kissed the Black Stone, and began to perform the seven rounds of *Tawaaf* (circumambulation). They said some insulting things about him, and this was repeated the following day. This time the heads of Quraysh leaped up together and encircled the Prophet, saying, "Are you the one who reviled our gods and said so and so about our religion?" "Yes, I am the one who said that," the Prophet replied. Then one of them seized him by the top of his garment. Here Abu Bakr interposed himself weeping and saying, "Would you kill a man for saying, 'Allah is my Lord'?" At this, they left him and turned upon Abu Bakr and dragged him along by the beard and head.

Hamzah Embraces Islam:

Hamzah, the Prophet's foster brother and his young uncle, was a man of tall stature, and of high standing in Quraysh. One day the Prophet was sitting outside the mosque near the Safa gate, when Abu Jahl passed by him. As the latter was hostile to the Prophet and to the new faith, he hurled a torrent of abuse at the Prophet, trying to bring him into disrepute, but the Prophet spoke no word to him, and returned home sadly. Within a little while, Hamzah arrived, with his bow slung over his shoulder, returning from hunting. When he was told of what Abu Jahl had done, he, fuming with rage, went out at a run to punish him. When he got to the mosque, he made straight for Abu Jahl; and, standing over him, he lifted up his bow and brought it down with all his force on his back, saying, "Will you insult Muhammad now that I follow his religion and say what he says? Hit me back if you can!" Some of the Makhzumites rose to their feet as if to help Abu Jahl, but Abu Jahl said, "Let Abu `Umarah (Hamzah) alone for, by Allah, I reviled his nephew with a right ugly reviling." From that day, Hamzah maintained his Islam and followed the Prophet's behests.

Quraysh Negotiate with the Prophet:

Quraysh now realized that the Prophet had become stronger, especially after finding a defender in Hamzah. This made it urgent for to figure out a way to stop the advance of the new faith, which, as it seemed to them, could only end in the damage of their high standing amongst the Arabs. A prominent leader of the Makkan oligarchy, `Utbah Ibn Rabee`ah, was authorized to negotiate with the Prophet. Gathering in the Ka`bah, `Utbah said to the Prophet, "O my nephew, you are as we know a noble of the tribe and your ancestors are high in our pedigree. You have brought to your people a matter of great concern, whereby you have rifted their community, ridiculed their ways of life, spoken shamefully of their gods and their religion, and even denied pure faith to their ancestors. So hear what I am going to propose, and see if any of this is acceptable to you. If it is wealth you seek, we will contribute to make you the richest of us all. If it is honor you seek, we will make you our overlord and promise to take no decision except with your consent. If, even, you think of sovereignty, we will elect you our king. And if this ghost which comes to you – meaning the revelation and visitation of Gabriel – is such that you cannot defend yourself against it, we will find you a physician and spend our wealth until you are fully cured." When he finished, the Prophet said, "Now listen to me, Abu Al-Waleed." He thereupon recited to him:

﴿حم {١} تَنزِيلٌ مِّنَ الرَّحْمَنِ الرَّحِيمِ {٢} كِتَابٌ فُصِّلَتْ آيَاتُهُ قُرْآنًا عَرَبِيًّا لِّقَوْمٍ يَعْلَمُونَ {٣} بَشِيرًا وَنَذِيرًا فَأَعْرَضَ أَكْثَرُهُمْ فَهُمْ لَا يَسْمَعُونَ {٤} وَقَالُوا قُلُوبُنَا فِي أَكِنَّةٍ مِّمَّا تَدْعُونَا إِلَيْهِ وَفِي آذَانِنَا وَقْرٌ وَمِن بَيْنِنَا وَبَيْنِكَ حِجَابٌ فَاعْمَلْ إِنَّنَا عَامِلُونَ {٥}﴾ (فصلت:١-٥)

"In the name of Allah, Most Gracious, Most Merciful. Ha-Meem. A revelation from (Allah), Most Gracious, Most Merciful - A Book, whereof the verses are explained in detail - A Qur'an in Arabic, for people who understand - Giving Good News and admonition: yet most of them turn away, and so they hear not." (Fussilat: 1-5)

The Prophet, peace and blessings be upon him continued to recite Allah's words until he ended saying:

﴿وَمِنْ آيَاتِهِ اللَّيْلُ وَالنَّهَارُ وَالشَّمْسُ وَالْقَمَرُ لَا تَسْجُدُوا لِلشَّمْسِ وَلَا لِلْقَمَرِ وَاسْجُدُوا لِلَّهِ الَّذِي خَلَقَهُنَّ إِن كُنتُمْ إِيَّاهُ تَعْبُدُونَ {٣٧}﴾ (فصلت:٣٧)

"Among His Signs are the Night and Day, the Sun and the Moon. Adore not the sun and the moon, but adore Allah, Who created them, if it is Him ye wish to serve." (Fus-silat: 37)

Thereupon, the Prophet, peace and blessings be upon him, placed his forehead on the ground in prostration. He then said, "You have heard what you have heard, Abu Al-Waleed; the rest remains with you." When `Utbah returned to his companions, they asked him what had happened. He said: "I have heard words the like of which I have never yet heard. It is not poetry, spells, or soothsaying. Men of Quraysh, hearken unto me and do as I advice. Leave this man entirely alone for, by Allah, the words I have heard from him will be blazed abroad." But they mocked at him saying, "He bewitched you with his tongue!" "This is my opinion," he said, "so do what you think fit."

Heads of Quraysh decided to negotiate with Muhammad and argue with him so that they would not be blamed for having left a way unattempted. So they sent word to him to come and talk with them. When the Prophet came, they began to repeat the same offers they had already made him before. When they finished, the Prophet said: "I am not possessed, neither do I seek honor amongst you, nor kingship over you. But Allah has sent me to you as a

Messenger and revealed to me a Book (the Qur'an) and ordered me to be a bearer of glad tidings and a warner. Even so have I brought you the message of my Lord, and have given you good advice. If you accept what I have brought you, that is your good future in this world and the next; but if you reject what I have brought, then I will patiently await Allah's judgment between us."

Having listened to these words, the negotiators requested that the Prophet ask his Lord to bestow on them gardens and palaces and treasures of gold and silvers, so that they might know his standing with his Lord and admit the truth of his mission. But the Prophet told them: "I am not one to ask of his Lord the like of such things, nor was I sent for that (purpose), but Allah has sent me to warn and give glad tidings." Thus the negotiations failed as the Prophet wanted nothing less than a complete submission to the new faith.

The Situation Grows More Serious:

The persecution of the Prophet and his followers was aggravated. Every clan that had Muslims among them started beating and imprisoning them, depriving them of food and water, and exposing them to the scorching heat of Makkah, with the aim of forcing them to forsake their religion. The

Prophet, peace and blessings be upon him, himself suffered various forms of torture and abuse.

`Abdullaah Ibn Mas`ood narrates: Once the Prophet was offering his prayers at the Ka`bah, when Abu Jahl was sitting with some of his companions. One of them said to the others, "Who amongst you will bring abdominal content (intestines, etc.) of a camel of Banu so and so and throw it on the back of Muhammad, when he prostrates himself?" The most unfortunate of them got up and brought it. He waited till the Prophet prostrated himself and then placed it on his back between his shoulders. I was watching but was hand-tied. I wish I had some people with me to stand out against them. They started laughing and falling on one another. Allah's Messenger remained in prostration and did not lift his head up till Faatimah (the Prophet's daughter) came and threw that (camel's abdominal contents) off his back. He raised his head and said thrice, "O Allah! Punish Quraysh." Abu Jahl and his companions were upset when the Prophet invoked Allah against them as they had a conviction that prayer and invocation were accepted in this city (Makkah).

Narrating another story of torture, `Urwah Ibn Az-Zubayr says: I asked `Abdullaah Ibn `Amr Ibn Al-`Aas, "Tell me about the worst thing the disbelievers did to the Prophet." He said, "While the

Prophet was praying in the Hijr of the Ka`bah, `Uqbah Ibn Abi Mu`ayt put his garment around the Prophet's neck and throttled him violently. Abu Bakr came and caught him by his shoulder and pushed him away from the Prophet and said, "Would you kill a man for saying, 'Allah is my Lord'?"

The First Migration to Abyssinia

The atrocities of Quraysh against Muslims escalated, so the Prophet, peace and blessings be upon him, advised them to migrate to Abyssinia (Ethiopia), saying, "If you were to go to Abyssinia, you would find there a king under whom none suffers injustice." So some of the Companions left for Abyssinia, fleeing with their religion. Having learned of their migration, Quraysh sent `Abdullaah Ibn Abi Rabee`ah and `Amr Ibn Al-`Aas, to Negus, demanding the deportation of the migrants back to Makkah.

Asked to clarify their position, Ja`far, the spokesman of Muslims, said: "Your majesty, we were people plunged into ignorance, worshipping idols, eating dead animals, comitting indecency, severing ties of kinship, and the strong would devour the weak. Then Allah sent for us a Messenger from amongst us, one whose lineage, veracity, trustworthiness, and integrity we all knew. He called us to the Oneness of Allah, to worship Him only and renounce the stones and idols we had worshipped. He ordered us to be truthful, faithful to our trusts, kind to our relatives, and to abstain from all that is not righteous. As soon as we believed in him, our people persecuted us and circumscribed our lives. So we came to your country hoping for protection."

The Negus asked Ja`far to recite some verses from the Qur'an, and the latter recited the opening verses of *Surah,* "Maryam " (Mary), which praise Jesus and the Virgin Mary. Negus wept until his beard was wet, and so did his bishops. He therefore refused to deliver the migrants to them, and the two envoys returned ignominiously to Makkah.

The Boycott

Then came even harder times. When Quraysh heard that the emigrants were comfortably accommodated in Abyssinia, that the Negus protected those who sought refuge in him, and that `Umar Ibn Al-Khattaab, one of their stalwarts, had converted to Islam, they grew more and more embittered and their hostility knew no bounds. Unanimously they decided to ostracize the Prophet's whole clan; the Hashimites, idolaters who protected them as well as Muslims who believed in him. A document was drawn up according to which it was forbidden for any one of them to hold any intercourse with that clan, sell to them or buy from them. This was to continue until the Hashimites outlawed the Prophet, or until he renounced his claim to Prophethood. The document was placed in the Ka`bah.

Wisely and quietly Abu Taalib took stock of the situation, and decided to withdraw to a valley on the outskirts of Makkah, where he and the Hashimites entrenched themselves. Deprived from everything for more than two years, the Hashimites and their supporters suffered untold hardships. Food was scarce; there was enough to meet their needs. At times they had nothing but the leaves of trees to sustain them. They lived in an ominous place where there was always the danger of a night attack.

However, the Prophet's courage and determination never weakened. He continued to go to the Ka`bah and pray publicly. He never doubted Allah's victory. Then came a breakthrough: five leaders of Quraysh, after the passage of three years of the iniquitous siege and boycott, felt guilty about unjustly isolating their kinsmen to perish in the valley. So they decided to tear the document and end the boycott. After he had a quarrel with Abu Jahl about the document, one of the leaders stepped into the Ka`bah and got the document. When he opened it, it was found that it was eaten by worms, all but the opening words "In Your Name, O God! " and thus the ban on Muslims was lifted.

Two Grave Events

That, however, was not the end of hard times and suffering. The Prophet soon lost his uncle Abu Taalib, the greatest benefactor to Islam. Thirty-five days after Abu Taalib's demise, the Prophet's beloved wife, Khadeejah, also passed in Allah's mercy. The Prophet was so deeply shocked by these two sad events that he called that year "the Year of Sorrow".

It was then, Ibn Hishaam states, that Quraysh began to treat the Prophet extremely offensively in such a way that they never dared do in Abu Taalib's lifetime. On one occasion, when the Prophet was coming from the Ka`bah, a young lout took a handful of dust and threw it in the Prophet's face and over his head. The Prophet went into his house with the dust still on his head and one of his daughters got up to wash it away weeping. "Don't weep, little daughter," the Prophet said, "Allah will protect your father."

The Prophet's Migration to At-Taa'if

With the growing hostility of Quraysh, preaching Islam in Makkah seemed hopeless. So the

Prophet decided to go to At-Taa'if, fifty miles southeast of Makkah, to seek help from the people of Thaqeef. Accompanied by his servant Zayd, the Prophet walked up the rugged mountains to that city. On reaching there, he met with their leaders and invited them to Islam, but even this city refused the heavenly message. Instead of welcoming the Prophet, people treated him harshly and stirred their slaves and louts to insult, shout at and hurl stones at him.

However, the Prophet was a rock of steadfastness and forbearance. In such a desperate situation, he took refuge in Allah and prayed: "O Allah, to You do I complain of my weakness, of me helplessness, and of my insignificance in the sight of people. O You Who are Ever-Merciful, You are the Lord of the oppressed, and You are my Lord. Into whose hands will You entrust me? Into the hands of some far off stranger who scowls at me? Or to an enemy whom You have empowered against me? If You are not angry with me, I do not care; but Your Clemency is wider for me. I seek refuge in the Light of Your Countenance whereby all darkness is illuminated and the affairs of this world and the next are rightly ordered, lest You may descend upon me Your anger, or lest Your wrath may beset me! It is for me to return to You until You are well pleased! There is no power nor might save through You." Then the Prophet gathered his strength and set off to Makkah again, still feeling confident of Allah's victory.

The Night Journey

The Prophet's plaintive supplication in At-Taa'if was answered. Allah willed to relieve him and let him enjoy the Light of His Countenance. While the Prophet was sleeping in his house, Gabriel, the angel, came to him and led him on a night journey on the Buraaq (a white animal, smaller than a mule and bigger than a donkey) to Jerusalem. There the Prophet led a host of Prophets in prayer. Then Gabriel ascended with him to heaven, where he saw the other Prophets of Allah. Finally, he reached the Lote Tree, which marks the knowledge of all creatures. There, Gabriel communicated to him the revelation in *Surah,* "Al Najm":

﴿إِذْ يَغْشَى السِّدْرَةَ مَا يَغْشَى {١٦} مَا زَاغَ الْبَصَرُ وَمَا طَغَى {١٧} لَقَدْ رَأَى مِنْ آيَاتِ رَبِّهِ الْكُبْرَى {١٨}﴾ (النجم:١٦-١٨)

"Behold, the Lote-Tree was shrouded (in mystery unspeakable!) (His) sight never swerved, nor did it go wrong! For truly did he see, of the signs of his Lord, the Greatest!" (An-Najm: 16-18)

In a famous *Hadith* narrated by Malik Ibn Sasaa', the Prophet said, "While I was at the House in a state midway between sleep and wakefulness, (an angel recognized me) as the man lying between two men. A golden tray full of wisdom and belief was brought to me and my body was cut open from the throat to the lower part of the `Abdomen and then my `Abdomen was washed with Zamzam water and (my heart was) filled with wisdom and belief. Al-Buraaq, a white animal, smaller than a mule and bigger than a donkey was brought to me and I set out with Gabriel. When I reached the nearest heaven. Gabriel said to the heaven gate-keeper, 'Open the gate.' The gatekeeper asked, 'Who is it?' He said, 'Gabriel.' The gate-keeper,' Who is accompanying you?' Gabriel said, ' Muhammad.' The gate-keeper said, 'Has he been called?' Gabriel said, 'Yes.' Then it was said, 'He is welcomed. What a wonderful visit his is!' Then I met Adam and greeted him and he said, 'You are welcomed O son and a Prophet.' Then we ascended to the second heaven. It was asked, 'Who is it?' Gabriel said, 'Gabriel.' It was said, 'Who is with you?' He said, ' Muhammad ' It was asked, 'Has he been sent for?' He said, 'Yes.' It was said, 'He is welcomed. What a wonderful visit his is!"

Then I met Jesus and Yahya (John) who said, 'You are welcomed, O brother and a Prophet.' Then we ascended to the third heaven. It was asked, 'Who is it?' Gabriel said, 'Gabriel.' It was asked, 'Who is with you? Gabriel said, ' Muhammad.' It was asked, 'Has he been sent for?' 'Yes,' said Gabriel. 'He is welcomed. What a wonderful visit his is!' (The Prophet added:). There I met Joseph and greeted him, and he replied, 'You are welcomed, O brother and a Prophet!' Then we ascended to the 4th heaven and again the same questions and answers were exchanged as in the previous heavens. There I met Idrees and greeted him. He said, 'You are welcomed O brother and Prophet.' Then we ascended to the 5th heaven and again the same questions and answers were exchanged as in previous heavens. There I met and greeted Aaron, who said, 'You are welcomed, O brother and a Prophet".

Then we ascended to the 6th heaven and again the same questions and answers were exchanged as in the previous heavens. There I met and greeted Moses who said, 'You are welcomed O brother and. a Prophet.' When I proceeded on, he started weeping and on being asked why he was weeping, he said, 'O Lord! Followers of this youth who was sent after me will enter Paradise in greater number than my followers.' Then we ascended to the seventh heaven and again the same questions and answers were exchanged as in the previous heavens. There I met and greeted Abraham who said, 'You are welcomed o son and a Prophet.' Then I was shown Al-Bayt Al-Ma`moor (i.e. Allah's House). I asked Gabriel about it and he said, This is Al-Bayt Al-Ma`moor where 70,000 angels perform prayers daily and when they leave they never return to it (but always a fresh batch comes into it daily).'

Then I was shown Sidrat-ul-Muntaha (i.e. a tree in the seventh heaven) and I saw its Nabk fruits which resembled the clay jugs of Hajr (i.e. a town in Arabia), and its leaves were like the ears of elephants, and four rivers originated at its root, two of them were apparent and two were hidden. I asked Gabriel about those rivers and he said, 'The two hidden rivers are in Paradise, and the apparent ones are the Nile and the Euphrates.'

Then fifty prayers were enjoined on me. I descended till I met Moses who asked me, 'What have you done?' I said, 'Fifty prayers have been enjoined on me.' He said, 'I know the people better than you, because I had the hardest experience to bring Bani Israa'eel (Children of Israel) to obedience. Your followers cannot put up with such obligation. So, return to your Lord and request Him (to reduce the number of prayers.' I returned and requested Allah (for reduction) and He made it forty. I returned and (met Moses) and had a similar discussion, and then returned again to Allah for reduction and He made it thirty, then twenty, then ten, and then I came to Moses who repeated the same advice. Ultimately Allah reduced it to five. When I came to Moses again, he said, 'What have you done?' I said, 'Allah has made it five only.' He repeated the same advice but I said that I surrendered (to Allah's Final Order)'" Allah's Messenger was addressed by Allah as such: "I have decreed My obligation and have reduced the burden on My slaves, and I shall reward a single good deed as if it were ten good deeds."

The next morning the Prophet told Quraysh of what he had seen. "How unbelievable!". They exclaimed, "the caravan takes a month to go Syria and a month to return, how could you do the return journey in one night?" When this question was posed to Abu Bakr, he said, "If he says so, then he is truthful. There is nothing to be surprised about. I believe him when he says that he received revelation from Heaven in an hour of the day or night. And that is beyond what you cavil at. "

The Prophet, peace and blessings be upon him, says, *"When Quraysh disbelieved me (concerning my night journey) I stood up in Al-Hijr of the Ka`bah and Allah displayed Al-Aqsa Mosque before me, and I started to inform them about its signs while looking at it."*

The Pledge of Al-`Aqabah

Meanwhile, the Prophet, peace and blessings be upon him, offered himself to the tribes inviting them to the Oneness of God and informing them of his Prophethood. One day he met with six men from Yathrib (Madeenah) at Al-`Aqabah. Then he called on them to embrace Islam, and they did. Then he asked them to swear to worship none but Allah, not to steal, not to commit *Zina* (illegal sexual relations), not to kill your children, not to utter slander, and not to be disobedient when ordered to do good deeds.

Then the Prophet, peace and blessings be upon him, said: *"Whoever amongst you fulfills his pledge will be rewarded by Allah. And whoever indulges in any one of them (except the ascription of partners to Allah) and is punished in this world, that punishment will be an expiation for the sin he committed. And if one indulges in any of them, and Allah conceals his sin, it is up to Him to forgive or punish him (in the Hereafter)."*

In the following year, twelve persons from the same city came and met the Prophet at Al-`Aqabah and gave him their pledge. When they left for Yathrib, the Prophet sent with them Mus`ab Ibn `Umayr to recite the Qur'an for them and teach them the principles and dictates of Islam. Then Islam spread far and wide in Yathrib.

The Second Pledge of Al-`Aqabah:

In the following year, at the time of pilgrimage, seventy-three men and two women from Yathrib came to Makkah in order to vow allegiance to the Prophet and invite him to the city. At Al-`Aqabah, the Prophet accepted their pledge on the condition that they protected and defended him as they would defend their own wives and children. Then one of their leaders stood up and said, "By him Who has sent you with the Truth (the message of Islam), we will protect you as we protect our wives and children. "

Migration to Madeenah:

Having heard the new of the success of Muslims in preaching Islam in Madeenah, the infidels grew more and more furious and began to inflict intolerable atrocities on Muslims. At that point, Makkah was no longer a safe place for Muslims to dwell in. So, the Prophet, peace and blessings be upon him, encouraged his followers to migrate and head for Madeenah. Only the Prophet, Abu Bakr, `Ali and those helpless noble souls, who had been detained in confinement or were unable to break free from slavery, remained there. When Abu Bakr asked the Prophet's permission to emigrate, the Prophet told him, *"Don't be in a hurry, for it may be that Allah will give you a companion."* Thus Abu Bakr understood that he must wait to emigrate with the Prophet.

A Plot to Kill the Prophet:

The time came for Quraysh to take effective measures with a view to stopping this tidal wave, and preventing the Prophet, peace and blessings be upon him, from migrating to Madeenah, then a stronghold for Islam. They had convened a meeting at their council chamber (*Dar An-Nadwah*), and decided to besiege the Prophet's house and put him to death. As Abu Jahl suggested, each clan of Quraysh was to nominate a strong, high-born young man, and at a given moment, those chosen men should together fall upon the Prophet and deal a mortal blow to him. Thus they would be relieved of him, and the blood wit would lie upon all the clans. The Banu `Abdu Manaaf, the Prophet's clan, would not be able to fight them all and, would therefore have to accept the blood money (*Diyyah*) which they would all contribute to. It was about this mischievous plot that the following verse was revealed:

﴿وَإِذْ يَمْكُرُ بِكَ الَّذِينَ كَفَرُوا لِيُثْبِتُوكَ أَوْ يَقْتُلُوكَ أَوْ يُخْرِجُوكَ وَيَمْكُرُونَ وَيَمْكُرُ اللَّهُ وَاللَّهُ خَيْرُ الْمَاكِرِينَ {٣٠}﴾(الأنفال:٣٠)

"Remember How the Unbelievers plotted against thee, to keep thee in bonds, or slay thee, or get thee (of thy home). They plot and plan and Allah too plans, but the best of planners is Allah." (Al-Anfaal: 30)

Gabriel came to the Prophet, peace and blessings be upon him, to forewarn him about the conspiracy they contrived against him and to advise him not to sleep that night on the bed he normally slept on. Before much of the night had passed, the assassins assembled at the Prophet's door waiting for him to sleep so that they might kill him. Seeing what they were doing, the Prophet peace and blessings be upon him, asked `Ali to lie down on his bed and wrap himself in his mantle. `Ali, who realised the risk he was taking, accepted the task with great courage and fortitude.

The Prophet then went to the house of his companion Abu Bakr. "Allah has given me a permission to leave the city and to emigrate, " the Prophet said. "Together with me? " said Abu Bakr. "Together with you, " replied the Prophet. Two camels were saddled for them, and they hired `Abdullaah Ibn Urayqit, who then had not yet embraced Islam, to lead them on the way. They handed over to him their two camels, which he kept and fed until the appointed time came.

Returning to his house, the Prophet told `Ali that he was about to leave for Yathrib (Madeenah), bidding him stay behind in Makkah in order to return goods which people had entrusted him with.

The assassins kept vigil all night long, waiting to fall upon the Prophet the moment he left his house, peeping every now and then through a hole in the door to make sure that he was still lying on his bed. The Prophet and `Ali were soon aware of their presence; and the Prophet took up a cloak in which he used to sleep and gave it to `Ali, saying, sleep you on my bed, and wrap yourself in this green cloak of mine. Sleep in it, and no harm shall befall you. Then the Prophet stepped out of his house casting a handful of dust at the assassins and began to recite:

﴿يس {١} وَالْقُرْآنِ الْحَكِيمِ {٢} إِنَّكَ لَمِنَ الْمُرْسَلِينَ {٣} عَلَى صِرَاطٍ مُّسْتَقِيمٍ {٤}﴾ (يس:١-٤)

"Ya-seen. The Qur'an, full of wisdom. Thou art indeed one of the Messenger, on a straight way. " (Yaseen: 1-4)

When he came to the words:

﴿وَجَعَلْنَا مِن بَيْنِ أَيْدِيهِمْ سَدًّا وَمِنْ خَلْفِهِمْ سَدًّا فَأَغْشَيْنَاهُمْ فَهُمْ لَا يُبْصِرُونَ {٩}﴾ (يس:٩)

"And We have put a bar in front of them and a bar behind them, and further, we have covered them up, so that they cannot see ", (Yaseen: 9)

the Prophet went out of the house and passed unperceived through their midst and went on his way.

The Trip to Madeenah:

As the day dawned, the assassins barged into the Prophet's house and to their utter surprise, found that the person lying in the Prophet's bed was `Ali, and not Muhammad, peace and blessings be upon him. This created a stir in the whole city.

On the other hand, Muhammad, peace and blessings be upon him, and his companion Abu Bakr proceeded to hide out in a neglected cave a few miles south of Makkah, on Mount Thawr. When they had gone a little way beyond the precincts of Makkah, the Prophet halted his camel, and looking back, he said: "Of all Allah's earth, you are the dearest place unto me and the dearest unto Allah, and had not my people driven me out of you, I would not have left you."

Reaching the cave of Thawr, Abu Bakr first walked in, plugged all the holes, cleaned it and then asked the Prophet to step in. They stayed in that cave for three nights. During that period, `Abdullaah, son of Abu Bakr, would go to see them daily after dusk and apprise them of the situation in Makkah. `Aamir Ibn Fuhayrah used to steal away unobserved every evening with a few goats to cover up the tracks of `Abdullaah and furnish them with a plentiful supply of milk. Asmaa', daughter of Abu Bakr, too came with a bag of provisions; but she had forgotten to bring a rope, so she took off her girdle and cut it into two, using one to tie the bag and keeping the other for herself.[2]

Abu Bakr was extremely afraid for the

[4]For this reason she earned the title "*Dhatu-Nitaqayn*", or the woman of the two girdles.

Prophet, peace and blessings be upon him. One day, the enemy reached the mouth of the cave and came so close to finding the two faithful souls. At that point, Abu Bakr whispered to the Prophet: "What if they were to look through the crevice and detect us? We are unarmed and at the bottom of the cave." Thereupon, the Prophet reassured him saying,

﴿لا تَحْزَنْ إِنَّ اللَّهَ مَعَنَا﴾ (التوبة: ٤٠)

"Have no fear, for Allah is with us." (At-Tawbah: 40)

Then the Prophet said to him, "What do you think of two when Allah is their third? "

Quraysh, on the other hand, were quite baffled and exasperated. A price was set upon the Prophet's head. Quraysh offered a hundred camels as a reward for whoever would seize Muhammad, peace and blessings be upon him and bring him back. This had spurred many to try their luck. Among those who were on the lookout for the Prophet and his companion in order to win the reward was Suraqah Ibn Malik. He, as Ibn Al-Qayyim narrates, received information that a party of four had been spotted on a certain route. So he decided to pursue it secretly so that he alone would be the winner of the reward. He mounted a swift horse and went in pursuit of the Prophet and Abu Bakr. On the way, the horse stumbled and Suraaqah fell on the ground.

Afterwards, he resumed the chase. He was once again curbed the same way, but the lust for material gain made him pay no heed to it. Again he swung himself into the saddle and galloped on at a breakneck speed till he came quite close to the Prophet. Abu Bakr's heart agitated and told the Prophet, "O Messenger of Allah, we are done for. " But the Prophet said, "Be not cast down, for Allah is certainly with us."

The repeated stumbling of Suraqah's horse and his falling to the ground made him realize that the Prophet was protected against him, and that it was a constant warning from Allah because of his evil design against the Prophet, peace and blessings be upon him. His heart immediately changed and the sworn enemy turned into an honest believer. Approaching the Prophet with a penitent heart, Suraaqah begged of him forgiveness in all humility. The Prophet forgave him and confirmed it with a token written by Abu Bakr on a piece of parchment. Then Suraaqah hurried back to Makkah and tried to foil the attempts of those who went out in pursuit of the Prophet and his companion

The Prophet Establishes the Muslim State

The Prophet Arrives at Madeenah:

In Madeenah, people were eagerly expecting the Prophet's arrival. They would go out every morning beyond the fields and palm groves onto the lava tract. After they had gone some distance they would stop and wait until the heat of the sun became unbearable; they would then return to their homes. One day they had gone out as usual and after a long tiring watch, they retired to the city. Then a Jew, catching a glimpse of three travelers winding their way to Madeenah, called at the top of his voice: "O Sons of Qaylah, he has come, he has come! " The voice was immediately taken up, and men, women and children went out hurriedly to greet the Prophet, peace and blessings be upon him, while chanting:

The White Moon[3] has risen over us,
Coming from the valley of Wadaa`.
Thus we must all show gratefulness
So long as there's one to call to Allah.
O you who've been raised amongst us
Obeyed all that you have conveyed.
You've come to give this city nobleness.
Welcome, O best caller to Allah.

[5] Meaning the Prophet, peace and blessings be upon him.

The Prophet, peace and blessings be upon him, stayed three days in Qubaa', during which he laid the foundations of his mosque, the first to be built in Islam, and which has been praised in the Qur'an in the following verse:

﴿لَمَسْجِدٌ أُسِّسَ عَلَى التَّقْوَى مِنْ أَوَّلِ يَوْمٍ أَحَقُّ أَن تَقُومَ فِيهِ فِيهِ رِجَالٌ يُحِبُّونَ أَن يَتَطَهَّرُوا وَاللَّهُ يُحِبُّ الْمُطَّهِّرِينَ {١٠٨}﴾ (التوبة:١٠٨)

"There is a mosque whose foundation was laid for the first day on piety; it is more worthy of thy standing forth (for prayer) therein. In it are men who love to be purified; and Allah loveth those who make themselves pure. " (At-Tawbah: 108)

On Friday he set out to Madeenah amidst cordial greetings of his Madinite followers who lined his path. At noon, he halted at a place in the Vale of Banu Salim Ibn `Awf, where he performed the *Jum`ah* prayer (i.e. Friday congregational prayer) and delivered the first *Khutbah* (i.e. sermon) in Islam.

After leading the *Jum`ah* prayer, the Prophet resumed his journey towards Madeenah. People of Madeenah came streaming forth, and vied with one another to invite the Prophet to their homes. Each and every one was anxious to receive him and said,

"Alight here, O Messenger of Allah, for we have strength and protection for you, and abundance." More than once did a man or a group of men belonging to the same clan take hold of the halter of the Prophet's mount Al-Qaswaa'. But each time the Prophet said, "Let her go her way, for she is commanded by Allah. Wherever she stops will be my abode."

The mount moved onward until she stopped before the house of Abu Ayyoob Al-Ansaari. The fortunate host stepped forward with unbounded joy for the Divine Blessing Allah bestowed on him, welcomed the Prophet and requested him to enter his house. Abu Ayyoob, out of the profound respect that he had for the Prophet, offered to vacate the upper storey, but the Prophet preferred the lower one, being more accessible to his visitors

The Building of the Mosque

The first task which the Prophet, peace and blessings be upon him, undertook in Madeenah was to build a mosque. He gave orders that it should be built where his mount knelt. He purchased the place from two orphans belonging to the *Ansaar*. Part of the land was a graveyard for the polytheists, where some graves were still unleveled. There were some date-palm trees there, too. The Prophet, peace and blessings be upon him, ordered that the graves of the polytheists be dug out, the unleveled land leveled and the date-palm trees cut down. The staunch Muslims immediately fell to work. They vertically aligned the cut date-palm trees towards the *Qiblahh*[4] of the mosque, as a wall, and built two stone side-walls for the mosque. The Companions of the Prophet would fetch the stones while reciting some poetic verses. The Prophet worked side by side with the *Ansaar* and *Muhaajiroon*[5] to construct the mosque. He never even hesitated to carry stones on his back and helped in setting them in proper place, while chanting:

> There is no life but the life of the Hereafter
> O Allah! Forgive the *Ansaar* and *Muhaajiroon*

Al-Bukhari reports on the authority of Anas Ibn Malik, may Allah be pleased with him, that the Prophet, peace and blessings be upon him, used to offer prayer whenever prayer was due, regardless of where he was. He would pray even in the folds of sheep. Then he ordered that the mosque be built. He sent for the chiefs of Banu An-Najjar, and told them,

[6] The direction to which Muslims turn in prayer.

[7] *Al- Ansaar* is the title given to the Muslims of Madeenah, whereas *Al-Muhaajiroon* is that given to Muslims of Makkah.

"O Banu An-Najjar! Name whatever price you wish for this garden of yours." They replied, "No! By Allah, we do not demand its price except from Allah." In that garden, there were graves of pagans, unleveled land with holes and pits etc., as well as date-palm trees. The Prophet ordered that the graves of the pagans be dug up, the unleveled land leveled and the date-palm trees cut down. The trunks of the trees were thereupon arranged so as to form the wall facing the *Qiblah*. Stone pillars were built at the sides of its gate. The Companions of the Prophet used to carry the stones reciting some lyrics. The Prophet joined them both in working and chanting. They would say, "O Allah! There is no good but the good of the Hereafter, so bestow victory on the *Ansaar* and *Muhaajiroon*."

Establishing Brotherhood among Muslims:

Just as the Prophet, peace and blessings be upon him, built the mosque in order to be a center of the new Muslim community, he instituted a pact of brotherhood between the *Ansaar* and *Muhaajiroon*, with a view to uniting the community of the believers still further. That was a necessary step since the Muslims of Makkah, who had left their homes and bid their friends and relative goodbye, were overcome by a sad feeling of loneliness. This pact of brotherhood was thus to help them cast off their loneliness and attune to the changed circumstances.

According to the new pact, when either of the two Muslims who had been paired as brothers passed away, his property was to be inherited by his brother-in-faith. This practice continued until the Battle of Badr, when Allah, exalted be He, revealed: *"And those who accept Faith subsequently, and emigrate, and fight for the Faith in your company, - they are of you. But kindred by blood have prior rights against each other in the Book of Allah. "Verily Allah is well-acquainted with all things. "* (Al-Anfaal: 75) The regular rule of inheritance, after the revelation of this verse, was allowed to take its usual course.

Such brotherhood was unique in the history of the world. It was so strong that it surpassed blood relationships. Al-Bukhari narrates that when Muslims came to Madeenah, the Prophet, peace and blessings be upon him, established a bond of brotherhood between `Abdur-Rahmaan Ibn `Awf and Sa`d Ibn Ar-Rabee`. Sa`d Ibn Ar-Rabee` told his brother, "I am the richest among the *Ansaar*, so I will give you half of my wealth. I have two wives, you may look at them and I will divorce whichever of the two you may choose, so that, after the expiry of her *`Iddah* [6], you may marry her. " `Abdur-Rahmaan replied, "I

[8]The period which a woman has to wait before she can remarry in order to verify that she is not pregnant, or out of mourning for her deceased husband.

am not in need of all that. Kindly direct me to the market so that I may earn my own fortune." `Abdur-Rahmaan headed for the market the following day and brought some dried buttermilk (yogurt) and butter, and then began frequenting the market since then. Few days later, `Abdur-Rahmaan came with traces of yellow (scent) on his body. The Prophet, peace and blessings be upon him, asked him whether he had got married. He replied in the affirmative. The Prophet said, "Whom have you married?" He replied, "A woman from the *Ansaar*." Then the Prophet asked, "How much did you pay her?" He replied, " (I gave her) a piece of gold equal in weight to a date stone (or a date stone of gold)!" The Prophet said, "Hold a wedding banquet (*Waleemah*) even if over one sheep."

Abu Hurayrah also narrates that the *Ansaar* once came to the Prophet, peace and blessings be upon him, to request that their orchards be distributed equally among Muslims of Madeenah and their Makkan brethren. But the Prophet, peace and blessings be upon him, was reluctant to have them shoulder this heavy burden. It was, however, decided that the *Muhaajiroon* would work in the orchards along with the *Ansaar* and the yield would be divided equally amongst them.

It is worth mentioning that by infusing such

spirit of brotherhood and selflessness in his followers, the Prophet, peace and blessings be upon him, wiped out traces of the long-established enmity among different tribes and clans, particularly the *Aws* and *Khazraj*.

Friendly Relation with the Jews

The Prophet, peace and blessings be upon him, then sought to establish friendly relations between the Muslims and the Jews of Madeenah, particularly those of Banu An-Nadeer, Banu Quraizah and Banu Qaynuqaa`. He made a covenant of mutual obligations, forming them into a single community but allowing for differences between the two religions. Here are some of its provisions, which would clearly give an idea of the rights of non-Muslims in a Muslim state:

- Muslims of Quraysh and Yathrib, and those who followed them and labored with them are one *Ummah* (community), to the exclusion of other people.
- Emigrants of Quraysh shall unite to pay the blood money among themselves, and shall redeem their prisoners with the kindness and justice common among believers.

Believers shall not leave anyone among them destitute (*Mufrah*) by not paying his redemption money or indemnity in kindness.

- Whoever is rebellious or seeks to spread enmity, or

sin, or injustice, or corruption among the believers, the hand of every pious Muslim shall be against him, even if he be his son.

Allah's protection (*Dhimah*) is one that is (and is equally) extended to the humblest of the believers.

- Believers are supported by each other.

- Whosoever of the Jews follows us (the believers) shall have aid and succor; they shall not be wronged, nor shall their enemies be helped.

- The peace of the believers is indivisible. No separate peace shall be made when believers are fighting in the Cause of Allah. Conditions must be fair and equitable to all.

- Believers must avenge the blood of one another shed in the cause of Allah.

- Whosoever kills a believer for any just cause shall be subject to retaliation unless the next of kin is satisfied (with blood-money), and the believers shall be against him as one man, and they are bound to take action against him.

- It shall be unlawful for a believer who abides by what is in this document and believes in Allah and the Judgment Day to neither help a criminal (*Muhdith*) nor give him refuge. And whosoever helps him or gives him refuge shall incur Allah's curse and wrath on the Day of Resurrection, and neither repentance nor ransom will be accepted from him.

- Whenever you differ about a matter, it must be referred to Allah and to Muhammad, peace and blessings be upon him.

- The Jews shall contribute to the cost of war so long as they are fighting alongside the believers.
- The Jews of Banu `Awf are one community with the believers. To the Jews is their religion, and to the Muslims is their religion; those who behave unjustly and sinfully will not hurt but themselves and their families.
- The Jews must bear their expenses and the Muslims theirs. Each must help the other against whoever attacks people of this document.
- They (all parties involved in the covenant) must seek mutual advice and consultation, promote righteousness not sin.
- The oppressed must be helped.
- A man is not to be held accountable for his ally's misdeeds.

The Change of Qiblah7

Till then, the Prophet, peace and blessings be upon him, used to pray with his face turned to Jerusalem. The Jews imagined that he was thus explicitly leaning towards Judaism and that he stood in need of instruction. The Prophet received a Divine command to change the *Qiblah* from Jerusalem to the Ka`bah at Makkah. It is said that the change took

[9] *Qiblah* means the direction to which Muslims in *Salaah* (Prayer).

place on Sha`baan, 2 AH (February, 624 AC).

This was a change of far-reaching importance, and it gave rise to different reactions in different circles. It strengthened the Muslims' loyalty to their faith and their Messenger. They expressed their faith in Muhammad as the recipient of Divine revelation and accepted the change most willingly. The Jews, on the other hand, were indignant and tauntingly said: "Muhammad, in changing the *Qiblah*, has opposed all earlier Prophets. Were he a real Prophet, he would not do like that. " The hypocrites, Ibn Al-Qayyim narrates, said: "We are not sure in which direction the Prophet wants to turn for prayer. If the previous position was right, he has abandoned it; and if this new position is right, it means that he had erred before. "

Referring to these different objections, Allah the Almighty says:

﴿سَيَقُولُ السُّفَهَاء مِنَ النَّاسِ مَا وَلاَّهُمْ عَن قِبْلَتِهِمُ الَّتِي كَانُواْ عَلَيْهَا قُل لِّلّهِ الْمَشْرِقُ وَالْمَغْرِبُ يَهْدِي مَن يَشَاء إِلَى صِرَاطٍ مُّسْتَقِيمٍ {١٤٢} وَكَذَلِكَ جَعَلْنَاكُمْ أُمَّةً وَسَطًا لِّتَكُونُواْ شُهَدَاء عَلَى النَّاسِ وَيَكُونَ الرَّسُولُ عَلَيْكُمْ شَهِيدًا وَمَا جَعَلْنَا الْقِبْلَةَ الَّتِي كُنتَ عَلَيْهَا إِلاَّ لِنَعْلَمَ مَن يَتَّبِعُ الرَّسُولَ مِمَّن يَنقَلِبُ عَلَى عَقِبَيْهِ وَإِن كَانَتْ لَكَبِيرَةً إِلاَّ عَلَى الَّذِينَ هَدَى اللّهُ وَمَا كَانَ اللّهُ لِيُضِيعَ إِيمَانَكُمْ إِنَّ اللّهَ بِالنَّاسِ لَرَؤُوفٌ رَّحِيمٌ{١٤٣}﴾ (البقرة:١٤٢-١٤٣)

"The fools among the people will say: "What hath

turned then from the Qiblah to which they were used? " Say: "To Allah belong both East and West: He guideth whom He will to a Way that is straight. " Thus have We made you an Ummat justly balanced. That ye might be witnesses over the nations, and the Messenger a witness over yourselves; and We appointed the Qiblah to which thou was used, only to test those who followed the Messenger from those who would turn on their heals (from a Faith). Indeed it was (a change) momentous, except to those guided by Allah. And never would Allah make your faith of no effect. For Allah is to all people most surly full of Kindness, Most Merciful. " (Al-Baqarah: 142-143.)

The Prophet on the Battlefield

The Great Battle of Badr:

When Quraysh came to learn that the Prophet, peace and blessings be upon him, was safe in Madeenah, out of their reach, and that his religion was spreading speedily, they started desperately preparing for an all-out attack in order to exterminate the nascent power of Islam.

It so happened that in the second year after the Hijrah, the Prophet, peace and blessings be upon him, received news that Abu Sufyaan Ibn Harb was heading home from Syria leading a large caravan of Quraysh, containing their merchandise. The Prophet called on Muslims to go out and intercept its passage so that they might compensate for the loss and properties they left behind in Makkah. Abu Sufyaan, on learning of the intention of Muslims, lead his caravan off the main route, and sent Damdam Ibn `Amr Al-Ghifaari to call Quraysh to defend their merchandise. Upon reaching Quraysh, Damdam cried: "Men of Quraysh, the transport camels, the transport camels! Your goods which are with Abu Sufyaan! Muhammad and his Companions are lurking, lying in ambush for them! Help! Help! "

The effect of this clamor and commotion was

instantaneous. An army of about a thousand men, a hundred cavalrymen and a large supply caravan, was quickly mustered. The excited throng of soldiers proceeded, under the leadership of Abu Jahl, to avenge the rumored deaths of all those who had been with the caravan.

Then came the news that Quraysh had set out to rescue their caravan, and that Abu Jahl was on his way spearheading a large army. The Prophet, peace and blessings be upon him, felt bound to apprise his followers of the gravity of the situation and consult them to let theirs be the choice between advancing and retreating. Abu Bakr and `Umar, may Allah be pleased with them both, spoke for the *Muhaajiroon* in favor of advancing. Then Al-Miqdaad Ibn `Amr rose to his feet and said: "O Messenger of Allah, proceed where Allah directs you to, for we are with you. We will not say unto you as the children of Israel said unto Moses,

"Go thou, and thy Lord, and fight ye two while we sit here" (Al-Ma'idah: 24),

but we will say: Go you and your Lord and fight, and we will fight along with you. " The Prophet thanked him and blessed him. He then asked the *Ansaar* to give him advice. Thereupon, Sa`d Ibn Mu`aadh rose to his feet and said: "O Messenger of Allah, we repose faith in you and believe what you have vouchsafed to us, and we bear witness that what you have brought us is the truth, and we have given you our binding oaths to hear and obey. So do whatever you like, and we are with you. By Him Who has sent you with the truth, if you should bid us cross yonder the sea and plunge into it ourselves, we would plunge into it with you, no man would stay behind. Neither are we averse from encountering our enemy tomorrow. We are well tried in war and trustworthy in combat. It may be that Allah will show you prowess of ours such as shall bring coolness to your eyes. So lead us on with the blessing of Allah."

The Prophet rejoiced at Sa`d's words and was really impressed by the fidelity and spirit of sacrifice which his Companions showed at this critical juncture. He said to them: "Go forward and be of good cheer, for Allah has promised me one of the two parties, even now, by Allah, it is as though I can see the places where the enemies would be killed."

Abu Sufyaan, on seeing that the caravan had escaped unscathed, sent word to Quraysh asking them to go back to Makkah, but Abu Jahl vehemently objected, saying: "By God, we will not return until we have been at Badr. Three days will we stay there; we will slaughter camels and feast and make flow the wine and singers shall sing for us, and the Arabs will hear how we marched forth and learn of our mighty gathering, and they will stand in awe of us forever. Onwards to Badr! "

The Prophet, peace and blessings be upon him, knew that it was imperative to reach the waters of Badr before the enemy did, so he ordered an immediate advance. On reaching the water of Badr, the Prophet ordered a halt at the first well the Muslims came to. Thereupon, Al-Hubaab Ibn Al-Mundhir came to him and said: "O Messenger of Allah, is this a place which Allah ordered you to occupy, so that we should neither advance nor retreat from it, or it is a matter of opinion and military tactics? " The Prophet, peace and blessings be upon him, replied that it was merely a matter of opinion and military tactics, whereupon Al-Hubab said: "This is not the place to halt, but take us on until we come to that one of the large wells which is nearest the enemy. Let us halt there and stop up the wells that lie beyond it and make for ourselves a cistern so that we may have plenty of water. Then we could fight their enemy who would have nothing to drink. " The Prophet at once agreed and Al-Hubab's plan was carried out to the letter. Then, Sa'd Ibn Mu`aadh said to the Prophet: "O Prophet of Allah, let us built a booth (of palm-branches) for you and put your riding camel beside it. Then will we encounter the enemy, and if Allah grants us victory over them, that is what we fervently desire. But, if not, then you can mount your camel and join those whom we left behind us. O Prophet of Allah, our love for you is not greater than theirs, and if they had known you were fighting, they would not have stayed behind." The Prophet thanked him, invoked blessings on him, and the booth was constructed.

It was Friday 17th Ramadan, 2 AH (17th March, 623 AC) that Quraysh marched forth and climbed the hill of `Aqanqal. When the Prophet, peace and blessings be upon him, saw them descending the slope into the valley of Yalyal towards Badr, he prayed: "O Allah, here come Quraysh exulting in their arrogance and vanity, contending with you and belying your Messenger. O Allah, grant the victory which you did promise me. O Allah, put them to rout this morning."

It was at Badr that the two parties came face to face. The battle broke out on Friday morning, 2 AH. The Prophet drew up his little army, arranged the ranks and exhorted the Muslims to fight in the Cause of Allah, saying: "By Him in Whose Hand the soul of Muhammad is, no man will be killed this day, fighting against them in steadfast hope of (Allah's) reward, advancing not retreating, except Allah shall straightaway admit him to Paradise."

Then the Prophet, in the company of Abu Bakr, returned to his booth and kept beseeching Allah: "O Allah, I implore you to fulfil Your covenant and promise. O Allah, if this small force (of Muslims) is vanquished, You will not be worshipped on earth." The Prophet repeated these words in such humility and pathos that his mantle slipped down his shoulders in a state of deep absorption. Abu Bakr, who was standing near by, consoled him thus: "Enough, Messenger of Allah! Allah will for sure fulfil for you what he has promised you."

Immediate was the response from Allah, Who sent down angels from heaven for the help and assistance of the Prophet and his Companions. Then the battle grew fierce, and the Prophet took a handful of pebbles and cast it at the enemy, saying: "Defaced be their faces." Then the battle ended in the crushing defeat of the disbelievers. About seventy men of Quraysh were killed and a similar number was taken as captives. Fourteen Muslims died as martyrs.

Then the Prophet ordered that the corpses of the enemies be thrown into a pit. The Prophet stood by the pit and said: "O men of pit, kinsmen of your Prophet, ill your kinship you showed him. Lair you called me, when others took me in; against me you fought, when others helped me to victory. Have you found it to be true, what your Lord promised you? I have found it to be true, what my Lord promised me.

" Some of his Companions wondered at his speaking to dead bodies, whereupon the Prophet said: "Your hearing of what I say is not better than theirs, only they cannot answer me. "

Then the Prophet, peace and blessings be upon him, consulted his Companions regarding the captives. `Umar was of the opinion that they should be killed, whereas Abu Bakr thought that it was better to accept a ransom and let them go their way. The Prophet, peace and blessings be upon him, agreed on the opinion of Abu Bakr and released the captives. But the verses of the Qur'an were then revealed in favor of `Umar's opinion. Allah the Almighty says:

﴿مَا كَانَ لِنَبِيٍّ أَن يَكُونَ لَهُ أَسْرَى حَتَّى يُثْخِنَ فِي الأَرْضِ تُرِيدُونَ عَرَضَ الدُّنْيَا وَاللّهُ يُرِيدُ الآخِرَةَ وَاللّهُ عَزِيزٌ حَكِيمٌ {٦٧}﴾ (الأنفال:٦٧)

"It is not fitting a Prophet that he should have prisoners of war until be hath thoroughly subdued the land. Ye look for the temporal goods of world; but Allah looketh to the hereafter: and Allah is exalted in might, wise. " (Al Anfal: 67)

The Jews of Banu Qaynuqaa` Break the Covenant

Following the battle of Badr, the Prophet, peace and blessings be upon him, assembled Banu

Qaynuqaa` in the market and addressed them as follows: "O Jews, beware lest you should call down upon yourselves the wrath of Allah which had just fallen upon Quraysh, and embrace Islam. You know that I am a Prophet who has been sent (by Allah): you find that in your scriptures and Allah's covenant with you." "O Muhammad," they replied, " be not deluded by that encounter with a people who had no knowledge of war, and the fact that you got the better of them; for by God if we fight you, you will know that we are the men to be feared. " The Prophet turned and left them, and they imagined for the moment that they had triumphed.

A few days later, at the same market place, an incident occurred which brought things to a climax. A Muslim woman came to the market to sell or exchange some goods, whereupon a Jewish goldsmith tried to provoke her. He tied the edging of her garment to her back, and when she got up, her private parts were uncovered. The Jews thereupon roared in laughter. A Muslim man, who happened to be present at the time, rushed to her rescue and killed the goldsmith. The Jews immediately fell upon him and killed him.

Within a few hours, the Prophet, peace and blessings be upon him, besieged them on all sides by an army which outnumbered their own until they surrendered unconditionally. Then `Abdullaah Ibn

Ubayy Ibn Salool went to the Prophet and approaching him he said: "O Muhammad, deal kindly with my confederates. " The Prophet paid no attention to him, and then when Ubayy repeated the same words he turned away from him, whereupon the latter clutched him by his coat of mail, thrusting his hand into the neck of it. The Prophet's face grew dark with anger. He said: "Confound you, let go your hold. " But Ubayy said: "I will not let my hold go until you deal kindly with my confederates. Four hundred men without mail and three hundred mailed protected me from the red and from the black[8]; would you cut them down in one morning? By God, I am a man who fears that circumstances may change. " The Prophet said, "I spare their lives. " He ordered that the Jews of Banu Qaynuqaa` should forfeit all their possession and be exiled. They then settled on the borders of Syria.

It is said that `Ubaadah Ibn As-Saamit, may Allah be pleased with him, allied with those Jews as had `Abdullaah Ibn Ubayy Ibn Salool. `Ubaadah went to the Prophet and, approaching him, he said: "O Messenger of Allah, I take Allah and his Prophet and the believers as my friends and protectors, and I renounce my covenant and friendship with the disbelievers. It was about him that the verse was revealed:

[10] I.e. all men whatsoever.

﴿يَا أَيُّهَا الَّذِينَ آمَنُوا لاَ تَتَّخِذُوا الْيَهُودَ وَالنَّصَارَى أَوْلِيَاء بَعْضُهُمْ أَوْلِيَاء بَعْضٍ وَمَن يَتَوَلَّهُم مِّنكُمْ فَإِنَّهُ مِنْهُمْ إِنَّ اللّهَ لاَ يَهْدِي الْقَوْمَ الظَّالِمِينَ {٥١}﴾ (المائدة: ٥١)

"O ye who believe! Take not the Jews and Christians for your friends and protectors. They are but friends and protectors to each other. And he amongst you that turns to them (for friendship) is of them. Verily, Allah guideth not a people unjust." (Al-Maa'idah: 51)

The Battle of Uhud:

The defeat at Badr was an ignominy which the pride of Quraysh could not leave unavenged. Revenge was, therefore, the catch-word all over Makkah. The disbelievers decided to wage a retaliatory war in the hope of breaking the back of Muslims. It was also decided that the profits of the escaped caravan headed by Abu Sufyaan should be devoted to providing equipment to the Quraysh army. Thus they mobilized an army of three thousand pitched warriors, seven hundred of whom were mailed soldiers, and two hundred well-mounted cavalry with three thousand camels and fifteen women, and then marched towards Makkah.

Receiving news of the advance of the Quraysh army, the Prophet, peace and blessings be upon him, convened a meeting in the mosque in order to discuss this issue with his Companions. He, peace and blessings be upon him, was of the opinion that Muslims should not fight, but if the enemy attacked them, they would engage in the battle in self-defense. But young Muslims, particularly those who did not participate in Badr, were eager to go out and encounter the Quraysh army. When the Prophet saw that it was the majority that supported fighting the enemy, he agreed to go for the encounter and commanded them to prepare for the battle.

After the prayer, the Prophet, peace and blessings be upon him, walked with Abu Bakr and `Umar, may Allah be pleased with them both, into his house to make preparations. Muslim men lined up outside and Sa`d Ibn Mu`aadh reproved them saying: "You have compelled the Prophet to go out against his will, albeit the command comes down to him from Heaven. Put back the decision into his hands and let him decide afresh. " In a little while, the Prophet, peace and blessings be upon him, stepped out of his chamber, clad in mail and helmet, his sword hanging from a leather girdle and his shield slung over his shoulder. Many of the men by that time had regretted the course they had taken, and said that he should do what the Prophet deemed fit and that they would follow him willingly, whereupon the Prophet told them: "It is not befitting a Prophet, after he has put on his armor, to take it off until Allah has judged between him and his enemies. "

Therefore, the Prophet marched out with an army of almost one thousand soldiers, among whom were only two horsemen and a hundred men in army. On the way, `Abdullaah Ibn Ubayy Ibn Salool, the chief of the hypocrites, along with three hundred, men deserted the Muslim army, thus reducing it to seven hundred, which was to face an army four times its number.

The remainder of the Muslims marched on until they reached the mountain of Uhud. There the Prophet, peace and blessings be upon him, drew up his little army and ordered them to stand in front of the mountain, so that they might be protected from behind. He then placed a batch of fifty archers and appointed `Abdullaah Ibn Jubayr Al-Ansaari as their commander. He said to them: "Don't leave your places; if you should see us conquer the enemy, do not leave your places; and if you should see them conquer us, do not (come to our rescue). "

Meanwhile the Quraysh army advanced. Abu Sufyaan commanded the center while the right wing was headed by Khaalid and the left by `Ikrimah. The encounter took place near the mountain of Uhud to the south of Madeenah.

In the first round of the battle, Muslims were victorious. Quraysh received shocks one after another with the fall of their warriors. The devoted Companions, such as Abu Dujanah, Hamzah and `Ali, Az-Zubayr displayed wonderful feats of gallantry against the overwhelming odds which stood unparalleled and created consternation and confusion within the disbelievers hosts.

At that point, the disbelievers staggered and took to their heels. Muslims followed them for a distance, but then occupied themselves with collecting the spoils. The archers on the top of the mountain too ran down from their position to collect booty. In vain did their commander `Abdullaah Ibn Jubayr remind them of the Prophet's order not to leave their posts on any account. They replied that the Prophet had not meant them to stay there forever. The battle was over then, they said, and the disbelievers routed. Only `Abdullaah and ten others remained in their positions, following the Prophet's commands.

The shrewd Khaalid Ibn Al-Waleed, cavalry commander of the Quraysh army, on seeing archers abandon their posts, seized the opportunity and led his men at full gallop to attack Muslims at the rear. The tide of the battle completely changed: many Muslims were slain, while others took to their heels.

The Prophet called on them to return, but their ears were deafened to his voice.

The Prophet himself, peace and blessings be upon him, sustained serious injuries: a sharp stone struck him in the mouth, gashing his lower lip and breaking one of his canine teeth. Moreover, two of the helmet rings pierced into his cheek. The blood began to run down his face and he began to wipe it away, while saying, "How can a people prosper when they have stained their Prophet's face with blood while he called them to their Lord? "

Then the disbelievers approached the Prophet to slay him, but Abu Dhujanah, may Allah be pleased with him, shielded him with his body. Arrows kept falling on his back. Also, Sa`d Ibn Abu Waqqas and Nusaybah Um `Imaarah Al-Ansaariyyah remained steadfast in their defense of the noble Prophet, peace and blessings be upon him. Ubayy Ibn Khalaf, furthermore, approached with a drawn sword, aiming at killing the Prophet, but before he could strike a blow, the Prophet had thrust him in the neck[9].

Among the Muslims who were killed in the battle of Uhud was the Prophet's nephew Hamzah. Before the battle, Hind Bint Abu Sufyaan sent word

[11] This is the only case the Prophet was narrated to have killed a person.

to Wahshyy Ibn Harb asking him to kill Hamzah, who had killed both her father and brother in the battle of Badr. When the battle grew fierce, Wahshyy kept watching the movements of Hamzah from behind a stone, and caught him off guard striking him with a javelin until he fell dead to the ground. Then he ripped open his belly, cut out his liver and brought it to Hind. She took it from him and bit away a piece of it, chewed and swallowed a morsel in fulfillment of her vow and spat out the rest. She then went to his see his corpse and on reaching it she cut off his nose and ears and parts of his flesh. Then she took off her necklaces and pendants and anklets and gave them to Wahshyy as a reward.

The Deportation of Banu An-Nadeer:

The Jews of Banu An-Nadeer had long been confederates of Banu `Aamir. The Prophet went to them to ask for their help in paying the blood money for the two men of Banu `Amir whom `Amr Ibn Umayyah Ad-Damryy had killed after he had given them an assurance of security. They agreed to what the Prophet requested. Despite the covenant between them and Muslims, hardly did they conceal their hostility anymore. They plotted to kill the Prophet. `Amr Ibn Jihash An-Nadryy volunteered to carry out the plot and went up to throw down a rock upon the Prophet.

While the Prophet and his Companions were sitting in front of one of their forts, Gabriel came to him and told him of their evil design. The Prophet immediately rose and left the company without a word, followed by his Companions, and returned to Madeenah. He explained to his Companions the treachery which the Jews meditated against him, and then sent Muhammad Ibn Maslamah to Banu An-Nadeer with the message: "By plotting to kill me, you have broken the pact I made with you. I give you ten days to depart from my country. Whosoever of you is seen after that shall be beheaded."

Most of them had already started preparing to leave, but Ubayy Ibn Salool sent word egging them on to remain and promising his support. So they sent to the Prophet telling him that they would not leave their possessions and their dwellings at any cost. Receiving their message, the Prophet said: "Allah Ever-Great. The Jews have declared war." Immediately the Prophet mustered an army and placed the banner in the hands of `Ali Ibn Abi Taalib, and then set off for Banu An- Nadeer, a little to the south of Madeenah.

At first they simply kept up an exchange of arrows and stones, relying on their forts. But when the Muslim army managed to besiege them on all sides, and their allies stirred not a finger to their aid, they were wise enough to leave. The Prophet allowed them to take anything they could carry on camels, except arms and armors. So they loaded their camels with all they could carry, and destroyed their houses so that Muslims might not make use of them. Some of them went to Khaybar and others headed for Syria.

The Battle of the Trench:

The Jews of Banu An- Nadeer who had been expelled from their land in the previous year settled in Jewish communities adjacent to Madeenah. It was only natural that they would seek revenge and incite tumult against Muslims. So, a number of their leaders, headed by Huyayy Ibn Akhtab, went to Quraysh in Makkah and invited them to join them in a joint attack on the Prophet in order to get rid of him altogether and put an end to his message. Quraysh enthusiastically accepted the invitation and said: "O Jews, you are the people of the first scripture and you know the nature of our dispute with Muhammad. Is our religion the best or his? " the replied: "Your religion is indeed better than his, and you are nearer the truth than he is."

Quraysh were highly delighted at those words and joined hands with the Jews to fight the common foe. Then the Jewish leaders went off to Ghatafaan and invited them to the fighting, and they too joined the confederacy.

When the Prophet, peace and blessings be upon him, heard of the intention of his enemies, he summoned his men to a consultation as to what would be the best plan of action. Salmaan, the Persian, suggested a stratagem as yet unknown to the Arabs: it was to dig a trench around Madeenah. He said to the Prophet: "O Messenger of Allah, in Persia when we feared an attack of horses, we would surround ourselves with a trench, so let us dig a ditch about us now. "The Prophet approved of his suggestion and the task of digging began. That was in Shawwal, 5Ah.

Many *Hadiths* show that the Muslims dug this ditch under very tiring conditions. They had to work with empty stomach exposed to the blasts of cold wind. The Prophet, peace and blessings be upon him, worked side by side with his Companions in digging the trench, and shared with them the pangs of hunger. Anas reported that the Prophet saw the *Muhaajiroon* and *Ansaar* digging in the cold morning. They had no slaves to work for them. When the Prophet saw how much hardship and hunger they were suffering, he said:

There is no life but the life of the hereafter
O Allah, forgive the *Ansaar* and *Muhaajiroon*

They said in reply,

We are the ones who've swore allegiance to Muhammad

To fight and strive in Allah's Cause as long as we live

Muslims had hardly finished the preparations when the formidable army of the confederates, consisting of ten thousand warriors, knocked all the gates of Madeenah with the determination to crush Islam. The whole of Arabia was thirsting for the Muslim blood.

Moreover, Huyayy Ibn Akhtab sought to induce the Jews of Banu Qurayzah, who had been allies of the Prophet, to renounce their pact with Muhammad and join the camp of disbelievers, promising them all kinds of concession and rewards. The Jews of Banu Qurayzah agreed and joined the hostile camp. When the Prophet heard of their renunciation of the pact, he was visibly troubled; and so he sent Az-Zubayr to find out the truth of the matter. When Az-Zubayr learned that it was true, he persuaded them to revert to the pact before it was too late, reminding them of the fates of Banu Qaynuqaa` and Banu An-Nadeer. But they were now confident of the victory, and so they said: "Who is the messenger of Allah? There is no pact between us and him nor is there any agreement. "

The allied forces with full supplies of arms and provisions had besieged Madeenah, while Muslims, hungry and weary, guarded the ditch day and night. They confederates made several attempts to draw the Muslims out from their trenches. Muhammad, however, resisted all temptation to fight the enemy, except on his own terms. Every attack on the moat was repulsed with a heavy loss to the confederacy. Now and again there was a rain of arrows, a charge of horsemen, movement of great companies of men – but, for all their stratagems, the Makkans and their confederates found Madeenah impregnable.

Then came Nu`aym Ibn Mas`ood, who had secretly embraced Islam, to the Prophet in order to declare his belief in him and bear witness to what he preached. He told the Prophet that he had friendly relations with both Jews and Makkans. "Messenger of Allah," he said, "bid me do what you will, for you have but to order me, and I will fulfil your orders. My people know nothing of my Islam." Thereupon, the Prophet tried a clever trick aimed at disparaging the disbelieving enemies. He said to Nu`aym: "Set them at odds with each other as much as you can. Say what you wish to draw them off from us, for war is deception."

Nu`aym went to Banu Qurayzah and told them that if Quraysh and Ghatafaan failed to inflict a decisive defeat on their enemy, they would return home and leave them at the mercy of Muhammad and his Companions. He advised them not to strike one blow for Quraysh until they gave leading men as hostages, in guarantee that they would not withdraw until the enemy had been overwhelmed. The Banu Qurayzah enthusiastically accepted his advice.

Then he went to Quraysh and told them that the Jews of Banu Qurayzah had regretted preaching their pact with the Prophet and secretly agreed together to take as hostages some of the leading men of Quraysh and Ghaṯafaan and give them to him so that he might cut off their heads. "So if the Jews ask you for some of your men as hostages, give them not one man of yours. " Then he went to his own people and other clans of Ghatafaan and told them the same as he had told Quraysh. So Nu`aym managed to sow distrust among confederates. Recriminations were on many tongues and the expedition had virtually failed.

For three days, after the prayer, the Prophet supplicated: "O Allah, Revealer of the Book, Swift Caller to account, put the confederates to rout, put them to rout and cause them to Quake. " In response to the Prophet's supplication, Allah sent down a piercing wind with torrents of rain which played havoc with the confederates camp. It blew for three days and nights so terribly that not a tent could be kept standing, not a fire burning, not a pot boiling, and men crouched shivering on the ground, huddled together for warmth. The confederates were in utter misery, and so they decided to retreat.

The Battle of Banu Qurayzah:

`Aa'ishah, Allah be pleased with her, narrates: "When the Prophet, peace and blessings be upon him, returned from the (battle of) the trench and laid down his arms and took a bath, Gabriel came to him while he was shaking the dust off his head, and said, 'You have laid down your arms! By Allah, I have not laid down my arms yet. Set out for them.' The Prophet said, 'Where to go?' Gabriel answered, 'Towards there.' pointing towards Banu Qurayzah, so the Prophet set out to attack them."

The Prophet ordered that none of his Companions should perform the `Asr Prayer except at Banu Qurayzah. The banner was given to `Ali and the Prophet set out with an army of three thousand fighters and thirty-six horses.

On the way, the `Asr prayer was due. Some of them said, "We will not pray until we have reached Banu Qurayzah, while others said, "No, we will pray at this spot, for the Prophet did not mean that for us." Later on, it was reported that the Prophet, when informed of what had happened, did not berate any of them.

The Prophet besieged them for twenty-five nights until they submitted to his judgment. The Prophet agreed to have Sa`d Ibn Mu'aadh, leader of the Aws tribe, to pass a judgment on them. Sa`d judged that their men (warriors) should be killed, their property divided, and their women and offspring taken as captives. On passing his judgment, the Prophet told him, "You have judged according to Allah's judgment."

The Treaty of Hudaybiyah:

It was about the sixth year of the Hijrah when the Prophet had a dream that he safely entered the Sacred Mosque with his followers and was performing the rituals of Hajj. Their heads were shaved and their hair cut short. As soon as the Prophet told his Companions of his dream, their hearts leaped up with joy since they had a longing desire to perform the Hajj and its hallowed rites after an exile of full six years. The Prophet asked his Companions to prepare for *`Umrah* (the lesser pilgrimage). So they marched forward carrying no weapons save sheathed swords, as they had no intention of fighting.

When Quraysh heard of the departure of the pilgrims from Madeenah, they decided to prevent them from entering Makkah, and immediately set out preparing for war. A large army was mustered and the roads to Makkah were completely blocked. When the Prophet heard of the determination of Quraysh, he said: "Alas, Quraysh! War has devoured them. What harm would they suffer if they let me and the rest of the Arabs go our own way? If they should kill me, that is what they desire, and if Allah should grant me victory over them, they would embrace Islam in flocks. If they do not do (i.e. embrace Islam), they will fight while they have the strength, so what are Quraysh thinking of? By Allah, I will not cease to fight for the mission with which Allah has entrusted me until He makes me victorious or I perish."

When the Prophet and his Companions reached Al-Hudaybiyah, some men of the Khuza`ah tribe came to him and asked him what he was there for. The Prophet said that it was not for war that he came forth. He said, "I have no other design but to perform `Umrah and pay a visit to the Sacred Mosque.

Then Quraysh sent `Urwah Ibn Mas`ood to try to persuade Prophet not to enter Makkah, but his attempt was unsuccessful. However, he returned to Quraysh very impressed by the unfathomable love and profound respect that the Companions showed him. He expressed his impression as such: "O people, I have been sent as an envoy to kings – to

Caesar and Chosroes and Negus –but never have I seen a king whose men so honor as the Companions of Muhammad do him. If he commands anything, they almost outstrip his word in fulfilling it; when he performs his ablution (*Wudu'*), they nearly fight for the water thereof; when he speaks, their voices are hushed in his presence; nor will they look him in the face, but lower their eyes in reverence to him. "

Then the Prophet sent `Uthmaan Ibn `Affaan, may Allah be pleased with him, to tell Quraysh that they had not come but to do worship and that they had no intention of fighting. Quraysh, however, were adamant and refused to give him permission to visit the Ka`bah. They offered him permission to perform Hajj in his individual capacity, if he so desired, but `Uthmaan said that he could not do so until the Prophet did. Yet, Quraysh kept him as a prisoner.

Muslims were anxiously waiting for `Uthmaan to come back, but his arrival was considerably delayed. Muslims were later informed that he had been killed. So, the Prophet told his Companions that they would not return to Madeenah until they fought the enemy. Muslims took a solemn pledge (Bay`ah) that they would sacrifice their lives to avenge the death of their Companion and would stand firm in defense of the Prophet. The Pledge has been called *Bay`at Ar-Ridwan* (the Pledge of Satisfaction). But soon came the news that `Uthmaan had not been killed.

When Quraysh saw the firm determination of Muslims to shed the last drop of blood for the defense of their faith, they came to their senses and agreed to conclude a treaty of peace with Muslims. According to the truce, the Muslims would go back to Madeenah that year, so that none of the Arabs would say that the Prophet made a forcible entry into Makkah. The Prophet agreed to the terms of the treaty.

The Battle of Khaybar:

Many of the Jews of Banu An- Nadeer and Banu Qaynuqaa` who had been expelled from Madeenah joined the Jews of Khaybar, a place situated about one hundred miles north of Madeenah. From there, they conducted their anti-Islamic activities inciting tribes and concocting plots to assassinate the Prophet. They made lavish use of their wealth to induce the neighboring tribes to take up arms against Muslims. They, moreover, thought that the Prophet would not fight them, as they were proud of the strength of their army of ten thousand warriors.

To forestall their hostility, the Prophet, peace and blessings be upon him, marched with a force of

1,400 men in Muharram, 7AH to Khaybar. When the Muslim army reached Khaybar and its forts became visible to them, the Prophet, peace and blessings be upon him, told his Companions to stop. Then he prayed: "O Allah, Lord of the heavens and what they overshadow, Lord of the lands and what they cause to grow, Lord of the devils and what evil they throw, Lord of the winds and what they winnow! We ask of You the good of this town and the good of its people and the good of what is in it, and we seek refuge in You from its evil and the evil of its people and the evil that is in it." Then he ordered his men to march forward in the name of Allah.

It was evening when the Muslim army were on the outskirts of Khaybar. The Prophet, peace and blessings be upon him, decided to wait until the morning. Should he hear a call to prayer (*Adhan*), he would hold back; otherwise he would attack. When the next day dawned, the Prophet heard no call to prayer. Thereupon he launched an attack on the fortresses of Khaybar. At sunrise, as land workers come out with their spades and baskets, they saw the Muslim army. They were put to flight crying, "Muhammad and his force! " Then the Prophet, peace and blessings be upon him, said, "Allah is Ever Great! Khaybar is ruined. "

The Muslim army managed to reduce the minor strongholds one after the other. With that task accomplished, they marched against Al-Khums, the main fortress of Khaybar. All accesses to the fortress were strongly fortified, and within the rampart was a well-equipped garrison. The Jews showed great courage and repulsed every attack on that fortress. Then the standard was given to `Ali Ibn Abi Taalib who was repulsed by the volleys of arrows which rained from the behind the parapets. It was indeed a tough fight. Muslims, however, were not dismayed. They dragged on the siege for twenty days and after constant struggle managed to take hold of the forts. Rich booty fell into the hands of the Muslims as the battle pulled down its curtain.

The Battle of Mu'tah:

In the year 6 AH, upon his return to Madeenah after securing the truce of Hudaibiyah, the Prophet, peace and blessings be upon him, sent messages to both Arab and non-Arab monarchs inviting them to Islam. The letters went to Heraclius, emperor of Byzantium, Chosroes II, emperor of Persia, Negus, king of Abyssinia, Muqawqis, ruler of Egypt and to some Arab princes who ruled over small cities bordering the two great empires. Among these letters was one sent to the king of Busra, to whom the Prophet, peace and blessings be upon him, sent Al-Harith Ibn `Umayr Al-Azdi to invite him to Islam. Unfortunately, the king was so arrogant that he considered the invitation to Islam an insult and responded by killing the Prophet's envoy.

The murder of the envoy was against all laws of inter-tribal morality. The Prophet was very much upset and shocked when the news of the death of his envoy reached him. So he ordered Muslims to prepare for war, and an army of about three thousand men was quickly mustered.

The Prophet, peace and blessings be upon him, nominated Zayd Ibn Haarithah to command the army and ordered that if Zayd were killed, Ja`far Ibn Abi Taalib would take the command, and if the latter were murdered, `Abdullaah Ibn Rawahah would replace him. The Prophet, peace and blessings be upon him, then ordered the Muslim army: "I advise you to fear Allah and be conscious of Him. Fight those who disbelieve in Allah, in the name of Allah and for His sake. Never should you breach a covenant, entertain treachery, nor steal from the spoils. Under no circumstances should you kill a new-born, a woman, an aging person, nor a hermit. Neither trees should be cut down nor homes demolished.

Then `Abdullaah Ibn Rawaaḫah encouraged warriors saying: "Men, by Allah, what you dislike is that which you have come out in search of; martyrdom. We are not fighting the enemy with masses, or strength or multitudes, but with this religion with which Allah has honored us. We have before us the certainty of either of two good things, victory or martyrdom."

War broke out. Zayd, may Allah be pleased with him, assumed leadership and began to fight in matchless spirit of bravery until he was killed. Ja`far, may Allah be pleased with him, then took the standard and tenaciously fought the enemy. In the thick of the battle, he dismounted, hamstrung his horse and resumed fighting until his right hand was cut off. He seized the banner with his left and that too was lost. He then clasped the banner with his bleeding arms until a Byzantine soldier struck him and cut him into two parts. Ibn `Umar, may Allah be pleased with them both, said that on the day of Mu'tah he stood beside Ja`far as he lied dead, and counted fifty wounds in his body, caused by stabs or strokes, none of which was in his back. Then Khaalid Ibn Al-Waleed, may Allah be pleased with him, assumed command, and Muslims rallied around him, and the advance of the enemy was checked, allowing an orderly retreat for the Muslim army. It was to Khaalid's credit that he made that safe withdrawal. Then Khaalid and the army returned to Madeenah.

The Conquest of Makkah:

According to the terms of the treaty of Hudaibiyah, Arab tribes were given the option to join either of the parties with which they desired to enter into treaty alliance. As a consequence, Banu Bakr joined the Prophet and Khuza`ah joined Quraysh. Banu Bakr, caring not a bit for the terms of the treaty, attacked Banu Khuza`ah. Quraysh supplied them with men and arms. One of the Khuza`ah tribe came to ask for the Prophet's aid and the Prophet promised help, saying: "May I not be helped if I don't help the sons of Ka`b (a clan of the Khuza`ah tribe).

The Prophet, peace and blessings be upon him, ordered preparation to be made for a foray. The expedition was first kept a secret but later on the Prophet revealed that it was to the city of Makkah that he wanted to lead his troop.

Under such circumstances, Haatib Ibn Abi Balta`ah, one of the trusted followers of the Prophet, sent a letter to Quraysh warning them of the intended surprise attack. He had given this letter to a woman who hid it in her hair. The Prophet, peace and blessings be upon him, then received news from Heaven of Haatib's action, and sent `Ali and Az-Zubayr after her and they forced her to hand them the letter. The Prophet summoned Haatib and asked him what had induced him to do that, to which Haatib replied: "Messenger of Allah, I still believe in Allah and his Messenger. But, I am a man who has no affinity of blood with Quraysh; my family is at Makkah and there is no one to look after it or to offer protection to it. " Here `Umar was about to cut off his head as a hypocrite, but the Prophet, peace and blessings be upon him, accepted Haatib's excuse and addressed `Umar thus: "He (Haatib) is one of those who fought in the battle of Badr. How do you know that he is a hypocrite, perhaps Allah has looked favorably upon the people of Badr and said: "Do what you wish, for I have forgiven you. "

After making full preparations, the Prophet, peace and blessings be upon him, proceeded to Makkah at the helm of ten thousand soldiers on the 16th of Ramadan, 8 AH. Muslims set for Makkah while fasting until they reached a place called Al-Qudayd, where they broke their fast. Then they resumed their movement until they encamped at a place know as Marr-Az-Zahraan.

The Prophet, peace and blessings be upon him, did not like to take Quraysh by surprise. Therefore, he ordered his men to kindle a fire on all sides for cooking purposes. The Prophet wanted to avoid bloodshed as far as possible and was anxious that the voice of reason would find its way through to the minds of the haughty Makkans hoping they would weigh the pros and cons of the matter before coming forward for an encounter.

In the meantime, Abu Sufyaan, Hakeem Ibn Hizaam and Budayl Ibn Warqah went out to gather information about the Prophet, whereupon some of the Prophet's guards saw them. He caught them and brought them to the Prophet. Abu Sufyaan embraced Islam.

Then the Prophet, peace and blessings be upon him, entered Makkah while on his mount and bowing his head until his beard almost touched the saddle, in gratitude to Allah. He entered his tent near the Sacred Mosque and offered eight *Rak`ahs* in thanksgiving. Then he entered the Sacred Mosque and performed *`Umrah* by making the seven rounds of the House. Then he headed for the idols which surrounded the Ka`bah, pointing at them with his staff, reciting the verse:

﴿وَقُلْ جَاءَ الْحَقُّ وَزَهَقَ الْبَاطِلُ إِنَّ الْبَاطِلَ كَانَ زَهُوقًا{٨١} ﴾
(الإسراء:٨١)

"And say: truth has (now) arrived, and Falsehood perished: for Falsehood is(by its nature) bound to perish."(Al-Israa': 81)

As he pointed at the 360 idols, one by one, each idol fell one after the other. Then he went to pray at the Station of Ibraheem; then to the well of Zamzam where his uncle `Abbaas offered him water to drink. Then he ordered that paintings inside the Ka`bah should be effaced. Next he went out and addressed the gathering in these words: "Praise be to Allah, Who has fulfilled His promise and helped His Servant and routed the confederates, He alone. " Then he asked the people: "O people of Quraysh! What do you think of the treatment I am about to accord to you? " They replied: "We say well, and think well: an honorable brother, and the son of an honorable brother. " To this the Prophet answered: "I speak to you in the same words as Joseph spoke to his brothers: *"He said:*

﴿قَالَ لاَ تَثْرِيبَ عَلَيْكُمُ الْيَوْمَ يَغْفِرُ اللّهُ لَكُمْ وَهُوَ أَرْحَمُ الرَّاحِمِينَ {٩٢}﴾ (يوسف:٩٢)

'This day let not reproach be (cast) on you: Allah will forgive you, and He is the Most Merciful of those who show mercy! (Yoosuf: 92) *Go your way, for you are free. "*

The Battle of Hunayn:

Two tribes, Hawazin and Thaqeef, about fifty miles to the south of Makkah, when receiving the news of the conquest of Makkah, made an agreement to fight the Prophet and attack him during his stay in Makkah before he could spread his religion throughout Arabia. Malik Ibn `Awf, the chief of Hawaazin, put forward a plan. He ordered his men to bring their families and belongings to the field, believing that their presence would best spur them on and they would fight to death in their defense. So they mustered an army of twenty thousand soldiers.

When the Prophet, peace and blessings be upon him, heard what the enemy tribes were planing, he ordered his men to make their preparations for war. The Prophet marched out with twelve thousand soldiers. It was one of the biggest armies that had hither to be assembled under the Prophet. So, some of the Muslims felt greatly elated with their numbers and with their preparations of war. One of them, out of excitement, said, "We shall not be worsted this day by smallness of numbers. " When the Muslim army approached the valley of Hunayn, they descended down the valley in the morning twilight. The enemy had reached it before them and hidden in its bypaths and narrow places in which they entrenched fully equipped and fully prepared. Then suddenly the enemy sprang from his ambuscade and charged furiously upon them. Staggered by the unexpected onslaught, one column after the other fell back and shocked the narrow pass. Panic then seized the Muslim army. Many of them turned and fled. It appeared that a general rout had taken place.

Amidst such adverse circumstances that befell Muslims with the exception of the Prophet's devoted friends and admirers, there was general chaos. The Prophet called out at the top of his voice: "I am the

Messenger of Allah undoubtedly; I am the son of `Abdul Muttalib." `Abbaas was also asked by the Prophet to call on the fleeing men; and he shouted at the top of his voice: "O Companions of the tree! O Companions of acacia! " They replied, "Here we are. " That was a turning-point in the battle; the fleeing soldiers tarried, formed their ranks and flung themselves at the enemy. The leader of Hawazin fought bravely, but was forced to flee with his men; and the women and children were taken captives. They were later returned to Hawazin.

Then the Muslim army marched to At-Taa'if, where the tribe of Thaqeef lived, and they besieged it for about three weeks. It was a fortified city and the inhabitants refused to surrender. The besiegers were received with showers of arrows so thick that they darkened the sky like the flight of locusts.

When the Prophet asked for Abu Bakr's opinion, it was given in these words, "I do not think you will gain from them this day what you desire. " Thus the Prophet ordered that the siege be lifted. Some Muslims asked the Prophet to invoke Allah's curse and Wrath on the city. Yet, instead cursing them, he raised his hands in prayer and said, "O Allah, guide Thaqeef, and direct them on to me." The prayer was answered and before long people of Thaqeef embraced Islam willingly.

The March to Tabook:

Soon after his return to Madeenah, Muhammad, peace and blessings be upon him, learned that the Byzantines had mobilized an army to invade the Muslim state in Madeenah. The Prophet told his followers to make the necessary preparations in order to meet the impending menace. They were hand-tied by a number of unfavorable conditions; the journey was long, the weather burning hot and there was a drought.

Those whose faith was frail were loath to quit the ease and shelter of their homes and pleaded inability on frivolous excuses. One of them said to the Prophet, "O Messenger of Allah, grant me permission to stay behind and do not tempt me, for every one knows that I am strongly addicted to women and I am afraid that if I see Roman women I shall not be able to control myself." The Prophet granted him permission and turned away from him.

However, the majority of Muslims responded to the call with usual readiness and zeal. Hardships could not demoralize them. They were very enthusiastic about fighting for Allah's cause. When the appeal was made for funds, voluntary contributions poured in from every quarter, as the leading Companions vied with one another to make generous donations. `Uthmaan, may Allah be pleased with him, contributed with three hundred camels and ten thousands dinars. `Umar, may Allah be pleased with him, presented half of his total belongings. Abu Bakr, may Allah be pleased with him, offered all that he had. Upon this, the Prophet asked him, "O Abu Bakr! Have you left anything for your family? " "Allah and His Messenger, "replied Abu Bakr. `Abdur-Rahmaan Ibn `Awf, may Allah be pleased with him, brought hundred ounces of silver.

But even such generous contributions did not suffice to meet the expenses of the expedition in hand. Some poor Muslims, who longed to take part in the expedition, could not make provision for it. So they came to the Prophet to be provided with mounts, but he said to them, "I can find no mounts for you. " So they turned and went home with their eyes streaming with tears as they could not find aught to expend.

Then the army of three thousand Muslims moved towards the north until it reached Tabook. They stayed there for about twenty days, but there was no fighting. The Prophet, peace and blessings be upon him, concluded treaties of peace with some of the rulers in the area, and returned to Madeenah.

When It Was Time to Leave

The Farewell Pilgrimage

In the tenth year of the Hijrah, the Prophet, peace and blessings be upon him, went to Makkah to perform the Hajj in the company of 30,000 Muslims on the 25th of DhulQa`dah. It took them ten days to reach Makkah. When he entered Makkah and saw the Sacred House, the Prophet prayed: "O Allah, increase this House in honor, magnificence, bounty, reverence, and piety. " He entered the Mosque and made the seven rounds of the Ka`bah, after which he prayed at the Station of Ibraheem. Then, going out to As-Safa, he shuttled between it and Al-Marwah seven times, and those who were with him did the same.

On the 8th day of the month of Dhul Hijjah, he rode to the valley of Mina and spent the night there. After daybreak, he rode to `Arafaat and it was at the base of the mount of *Rahmah* (mercy) that the Prophet stayed there the whole day. Then the Prophet addressed the pilgrims, saying: "O people, listen to my words. I do not know whether I shall ever meet you in this place after this year. O people, surely your blood, your property and your honor are inviolable until you meet your Lord, even as this day and this month are inviolable for all. Surely you will meet your Lord, and He will for sure ask you about your deeds. O people, have I faithfully conveyed the message? O Allah, be my witness.

He who has any trust with him let him return it to him who entrusted him with it. Verily, all usury is abolished, and you only have a right to your capital, without your inflicting injustice on others, nor others inflicting injustice on you. Allah has decreed that there should be no usury. And the usury of Al-`Abbaas Ibn `Abdul Muttalib is abolished, all of it. Surely all bloodshed in the pre-Islamic period is to be left unavenged. The first claim on blood I abolished is that of Rabee`ah Ibn Al-Haarith, who was nursed among Banu Layth and whom Hudhayl killed. It is the first bloodshed in the pre-Islamic period which I deal with.

O people, Satan has despaired of ever being worshiped in your land, but if he can be obeyed in anything short of worship, he will be pleased with matters you may despair and think of little account, so beware of him in your religion.

O people, postponement of sacred months is only an excess of disbelief whereby those who disbelieve are led into error; they hold it lawful (to fight in) one year and unlawful another to make up the number of months made unlawful by Allah. Surely time has completed its cycle and it is now as it was on the day Allah created heaven and earth. The number of months with Allah is twelve; four of them are sacred, three consecutive and Rajab, which is between Jumadah and Sha`baan.

O people, you have rights over your wives and they have rights over you. You have the right that they should not defile your beds, and that they should commit evident obscenity. If they do, Allah permits you to admonish them, refuse to share their beds, and beat them lightly. If they refrain from these sins, they have a right to their provision and clothing with kindness. Lay injunctions on women kindly, for they are the helpless without you, unable to provide for themselves. Surely you have taken them only as a trust from Allah and their private parts have been made lawful to you by the word of Allah.

O people, be mindful of what I say. I have left amongst you that which, if you hold fast to, shall preserve you from error, an evident indication; the Book of Allah and the *Sunnah* of His Prophet.

O people, listen and give heed to what I say. Remember that every Muslim is a Muslim's brother, and that Muslims are brothers. It is not lawful for anybody to take from his brother except what he gives him willingly; so do not wrong yourselves. O Allah, have I faithfully conveyed the message? " Then these verses were revealed:

﴿الْيَوْمَ يَئِسَ الَّذِينَ كَفَرُوا مِن دِينِكُمْ فَلاَ تَخْشَوْهُمْ وَاخْشَوْنِ الْيَوْمَ
أَكْمَلْتُ لَكُمْ دِينَكُمْ وَأَتْمَمْتُ عَلَيْكُمْ نِعْمَتِي وَرَضِيتُ لَكُمُ الإِسْلاَمَ دِينًا
{٣}﴾ (المائدة:٣)

"This day those who reject faith given up all hope of your religion. Yet fear them not but fear Me. This day have I perfected your religion for you, completed my favor upon you, and have chosen Islam as your religion." (Al-Maa'idah: 3)

The Prophet Departs to His Heavenly Abode

By that time, the Prophet's mission was completed. The time came for him to depart to his heavenly abode. He began to suffer from illness and his health deteriorated at an alarming speed.

Al Bukhari narrates that on the early days of Safar, 11 AH, the Prophet, peace and blessings be upon him, went to the graves of the martyrs of Uhud and offered prayer for them. Then he stood on the pulpit and addressed his followers: "I am to precede you and I am your witness. Your tryst with me is at the Fount[10], which verily I behold from here where now I stand. I have been given the keys of worldly

[10] This is the Fount (of abundance) which Allah mentions in *Surah, "Al-Kawthar"*. On Judgment Day, righteous Muslims will be allowed to drink from this Fount, after which they will not grow thirsty ever again.

treasures. By Allah, I do not fear for you that you will associate partners with Allah after me, but I do fear for you from this world, lest you should strike one another's necks for the acquisition of worldly gains."

It is also narrated that he, peace and blessings be upon him, went to Al-Baqee` cemetery and prayed for forgiveness for the martyrs, saying, "Peace be on you, people of the graves! Happy are you that you are so much better than men now alive. Dissension have come like waves of darkest night one after the other, each worse than the previous one."

On Monday 29th of Safar, 11 H., the Prophet went to Al-Baqee` and prayed for the dead. Then he returned to his wife Maymoonah's house. The fever grew violent and the pain considerably increased. But, withstanding all this suffering with remarkable calmness and serenity, he led prayer in the mosque. He then fell too week and his illness worsened. He set to his wives: "Pour over me seven skins of water from different wells so that I may go out to the men and exhort them." They had him sit down in a tub belonging to Hafsa and poured water over him until he cried, "Enough, enough!" Then they helped him get dressed and bound up his head and `Ali and `Abbaas supported him to go to the mosque, where he sat on the pulpit and addressed the people, saying: "There is a slave whom Allah offered the choice between this world and that which is with Him, and the slave has chosen that which is with Allah." It was only Abu Bakr who perceived what the Prophet meant, and so he burst into to tears, as he knew that the Prophet was speaking of himself and that the choice meant imminent death. The Prophet realised that his friend had understood, and asking him not to weep, he said: "The most bountiful of men to me in his companionship and his sacrifice of his wealth is Abu Bakr. If I where to choose a bosom friend, I would choose Abu Bakr - but companionship and brotherhood in faith remain between us until Allah unites us in His presence."

When the Prophet grew seriously ill, `Aa'ishah narrated, he ordered the people to tell Abu Bakr to lead them in prayer. But `Aa'ishah feared that it would greatly pain her father to take the place of the Prophet. So she said, "Messenger of Allah, Abu Bakr is a very sensitive man, not strong of voice and much given to weeping when he recites the Qur'an." To this, the Prophet answered, "You are even like the women that were with Joseph. Tell Abu Bakr to lead the people in prayer."

The Prophet lay much of the time with his head resting on `Aa'ishah's breasts or on her lap. His daughter Faatimah replied: "The first time, the Prophet told me that he would not recover from his illness and therefore I wept. The second time he told me that I would be the first of his family to follow him, and that made me laugh."

The malady of the Prophet assumed a serious turn. Fever rose to such a pitch that the hands could hardly be placed upon the Prophet's body because of the burning heat. His body was racking with pain; but he was too busy calling on people to righteousness. Turning to his wives who sat close by, he said: "O Faaṯimah, my daughter and you, S̱afiyyah, my aunt! Strive to do that which shall please Allah, for I verily have no power with Him to save you in any way."

On the 11th of Rabee` Al-Awwal, fever and pain had somewhat abated and there was some recovery of strength. The Prophet, hearing the call to prayer, decided to go to the mosque. The prayer had already begun when he entered, and Muslims were almost drawn away with the joy of seeing the Prophet, but he motioned them to continue. Abu Bakr had been conscious of the stir behind him, and he realized that the Prophet himself must have stepped into the mosque. So without turning his head, Abu Bakr stepped back, but the Prophet placed his hand on his shoulder and pushed him gently forward as a sign that he should continue leading Muslims in prayer. When he finished, the Prophet sat on the pulpit and addressed his devoted followers as such: "By Allah, I have not made anything lawful except that which Allah has declared lawful; nor have I declared anything unlawful except that which Allah has deemed forbidden."

The Prophet seemed quite exhausted, so he went back to `Aa'ishah 's house accompanied by two of his Companions. As the day advanced, his health failed rapidly. `Aa'ishah, seeing he was too frail, raised his head from the pillow and placed it on her lap. She kept moisturizing his forehead with damp cloth. The fever was very high. But the noble Prophet remained calm and never complained. He had resigned to the will of Allah and repeated the following words over and over again: "In the company of those on whom is the grace of Allah."

He felt as if he was drifting towards the inevitable end. Though going through the throes of death, he did not for a moment lose courage. He kept on supplicating Allah to help him: "O Lord! I beseech You seeking Your help through the agony of death."

At this point, `Aa'ishah's brother, `Abdur-Rahmaan, entered the room with a green *Siwaak* (a tooth stick) in his hand. Seeing that his eyes rested on it, `Aa'ishah knew that he wanted it. So she took it from her brother and chewed it a little to make it soft and pliable. Then she gave it to the Prophet, who brushed his teeth with it vigorously despite his sickness.

His strength now rapidly sank and he was heard saying: "Lord, grant me pardon and join me with companionship on high." He also a murmured, "Nay, the most Exalted Companion in Paradise." Then he said, "Prayer! The persons who have been entrusted to your care!" This he repeated several times. Then he began to lose consciousness and his strength ebbed back. His eyes opened widely and he said clearly: "Lord! Blessed is the companionship on high." His limbs gradually relaxed. He fell back in `Aa'ishah's lap. She fixed her eyes upon him anxiously, almost hoping to get a response from him but she found, to her great sorrow, that the faint suggestion of a smile which relaxed her husband's lips did not belong to this world. The Prophet, peace and blessings be upon him, by then had returned to the companionship of the One on high. That was on Monday 12th, Rabee` Al-Awwal, in the 11th year of the *Hijrah*.

When the news of the Prophet's death spread to all corners of the city, consternation blazed through the ranks of the people. Some wept bitterly, some were struck dumb, some disbelieved the news of his death and held that it was only a swoon. `Umar Ibn Al Khattaab stood up and said, "Some hypocrites think that the Prophet has died; but the Prophet is not dead. However, he has gone to his Lord as Moses, son of `Imraan, had gone to his

Lord, and he had been absent from his people forty nights, and he (Moses) returned to them after it was said that he had died. By Allah, the Prophet will return as Moses had returned, and he will surely cut off the hands and feet of men who allege that he is dead."

Just then Abu Bakr appeared passing through the mosque and disregarding the crowds that pressed about him, he walked onwards into the house of `Aa'ishah where the Prophet, peace and blessings be upon him, was lying. He uncovered his face and kissed him saying, "You are dearer to me than my father and mother. You have tasted death which Allah has decreed; a second death will never overtake you." He then went out while `Umar was still talking to the people, and he said, "Gently, `Umar, calm down." But `Umar did not listen to him. So Abu Bakr moved towards the people who had thronged round him and addressed them saying: "O people, let whoever worships Muhammad know that Muhammad is surely dead, and let whoever worships Allah know that Allah is alive and shall never die." He then recited the verse:

﴿وَمَا مُحَمَّدٌ إِلاَّ رَسُولٌ قَدْ خَلَتْ مِن قَبْلِهِ الرُّسُلُ أَفَإِن مَّاتَ أَوْ قُتِلَ
انقَلَبْتُمْ عَلَى أَعْقَابِكُمْ وَمَن يَنقَلِبْ عَلَىَ عَقِبَيْهِ فَلَن يَضُرَّ اللّهَ شَيْئًا
وَسَيَجْزِي اللّهُ الشَّاكِرِينَ {١٤٤}﴾ (آل عمران:١٤٤)

"Muhammad is no more than a Messenger: many were the Messengers that passed away before him. If he died or were slain, will ye then turn back on your heels? If any did turn back on his heels, not the least harm will he do to Allah; but Allah (on the other hand) will swiftly reward those who (serve Him) with gratitude." (Ali `Imraan: 144)

This short sermon brought solace to the wounded hearts of Muslims and they submitted with cheerful resignation to the will of Allah! `Umar said, "By Allah, when I heard Abu Bakr recite that verse, it was as if I had never heard it before, and I was dumbfounded so that my legs could not carry me and I felt to the ground knowing that the Prophet was indeed dead."

`Ali and `Abbaas undertook the task of washing the Prophet's body with his garment on him. As `Ali passed his hand over his garment, he said: "Dearer to me than my father and mother, how immaculate are you alive and dead!"

The Companions disagreed as to where to bury the Prophet, peace and blessings be upon him. Abu Bakr ended the problem when he recalled that the Prophet had said: "No Prophet dies but is buried where he passes away." Thus, the grave was dug in the floor of `Aa'ishah's room near the bed where the Prophet was lying.

People began to come in groups to offer funeral prayer for the Prophet, peace and blessings be upon him; first, his family, then the *Muhaajiroon*, then the *Ansaar*. Men prayed first, followed by women, then children. No man led people in prayer, and the burial took place Wednesday in the middle of the night. Amidst genuine feelings of profound grief and sorrow, the words of Umm Ayman most adequately expressed the reasons behind those feelings. "Not for him do I weep, "she said, "do I not know that he has gone to that which is better for him than this world? But I weep for the revelation from heaven which has been cut off from us."

May Allah's Peace and Blessings be upon you, O beloved Prophet, the best of Allah's creatures.

References

Arabic:

- Ibn Katheer , Al-Bedayah wan-Nihaayah, cairo, Dar At-Taqwa , 1998.

- Al-Mubarkafoori, Safyy Ar-Rahmaan, *Ar-Raheeq Al-Makhtoom,* Cairo, Dar Al-Fajr, 1994.

- Al-Booti, *Fiqh As-Seerah,* Beirut, Dar Al-Fikr, 1978.

- As-Sibaa`i, Mustafa, *As-Seerah An-Nabawiyyah Dooroos Wa`ibar*, Cairo, Daru-Salaam, 1998.

- English:

- A. Guillaume, *The Life of Muhammad* (a translation of Ibn Is-haaq's Seerat Rasulullaah), Ed, Oxford University Press, 1968.

- Lings, Martin, *Muhammad* صلى الله عليه و سلم. Allen & Unwin, London, 1984.

- Siddeeqi, `Abdul Hameed, *The Life of Muhammad*, Beirut, Dar El-Fath, 1969.

www.ingramcontent.com/pod-product-compliance
Lightning Source LLC
Chambersburg PA
CBHW062142160726
48282CB00027B/915
* 9 7 8 8 1 1 9 9 4 6 1 1 2 *